YOUR STEADY SOUL
May you transform your pain, anger, and hurt into wisdom, kindness, and love.

Leta B.

NOTE

If you feel you are in need of receiving expert services, please contact an expert in the appropriate field for treatment and/or advice. The book, *Your Steady Soul*, is sold with the understanding that the contents of the book are the author's experiences, beliefs, and ideas. The author is not rendering legal, psychological, financial, or any other expert professional services.

Your Steady Soul
Copyright © 2014 by Leta B.

All rights reserved. No part of this book may be reproduced by mechanical, photographic, or electronic process, or in the form of a phonographic recording; nor may it be stored in a retrieval system, transmitted, or otherwise be copied for public or private use – other than for "fair use" as brief quotations embodied in articles and reviews without prior written permission of the author, Leta B.

Leta B.
www.yoursteadysoul.us / leta@yoursteadysoul.us

> *Author:* Leta B.
> *Copyeditor:* Lisa Kimz and Eileen Bisgard
> *Cover design and illustrations:* Lisa Kimz
> *Cover layout:* Max Web Profiling, web design services
> *Cover photograph:* Leta B.
> *Author photograph by:* Max Web Profiling, web design services

Library of Congress Cataloging-in-Publication Data

B., Leta
　Your Steady Soul / by Leta B. -- 1st ed.
　　p. cm.
　ISBN: 978-0-9863440-0-8

　1. Spiritual life. 2. Humanity. 3. New Age movement. I. Title.

Library of Congress Control Number: 2014922218

Printed in the United States of America

To every person who has never experienced genuine love and kindness, may you still have the strength to find the love and light that exists within your soul to give, thrive, and shine.

Dear Alize,

May you let the beautiful light within you shine. May your future be filled with an abundance of peace, joy, and blessings. You have so much strength and wisdom within to keep you steady. I believe in you.

With much love,
~ Leda

Contents

Acknowledgements i

Introduction 1

A Love Letter from My Heart to Yours 5

CHAPTER 1 *Your Steady Soul* 7

CHAPTER 2 *Finding the Light Inside* 15

CHAPTER 3 *Transforming Pain and Hurt into Peace, and Receiving Blessings* 39

CHAPTER 4 *Awareness* 49

CHAPTER 5 *Aligning Mind and Soul* 59

CHAPTER 6 *What You Feed Will Grow* 71

CHAPTER 7 *Children Are Blessings Not Burdens* 83

CHAPTER 8 *Beyond Your Comfort Zone* 95

CHAPTER 9 *Intuition – Gift from the Divine* 101

Chapter 10	*Compass of the Soul*	121
Chapter 11	*Humanity*	129
Chapter 12	*Soul Print*	137

Quotes 143

Drawing: Your Steady Soul 147

Helpful Information 151

Acknowledgements

I have so much gratitude for so many special souls that have created soul prints in my life, and I wish that I could acknowledge all of them; however, I can only mention some by name. I want to thank the following special people in my life:

To Jason, we have been married for over 24 years, you are truly wonderful, thank you for all you have given me, and for the many years filled with love and precious heartfelt memories.

To our four precious daughters, you are all such strong beautiful angels on this Earth, and your strength in character will continue to set an example for many people.

To Greg and Kevin, you are so special and have so much to be proud of, thank you for your love and all you have given me.

To CF, you are beautiful, it is my wish that you realize your depth of wisdom, strength of spirit existing within you, and that you give your dear heart the well-deserved permission to soar.

To Irene, my other mother and friend, thank you for everything. Thank you so much for the love you have shown me over the years.

Thank you for teaching me that laughter during the difficult times creates light.

Much love to my nieces and nephews. Please let your beautiful light shine.

Cathy, you have such a generous heart. I am so grateful for you.

In loving memory of my dear Mother, she showed so much kindness to others while she was alive.

In loving memory of my dear sister Caryl, I hope your courage, reflected in this book, will help others while honoring your life. Gary, your work to connect to your steady soul in recent years reflects strength within you.

To Lisa, you are a beautiful wave of artistic creation, dedication, and boundless love.

To Wendy, you radiate an angelic light, and your steady soul is inspiring.

To Eileen, thank you for your friendship and for all your hard work to improve this world. You set an example by using your legal career to help the most vulnerable members of our society.

To Connie, you have a pure soul, and you have proven you have the strength to overcome a mountain of obstacles in your way.

Thank you to all of the precious children, who were abused and neglected, which I legally represented over the years. It is my prayer that you use the courage within you to transform your painful experiences into wisdom, and that you let your true colorful light shine.

To the amazing team from B&A, P.C., thank you for your hard work, dedication, and contribution to help so many clients. Please let your compassionate hearts shine.

To Carol, you have such a caring heart. Thank you for all of your support and love.

To Barbara, thank you for believing in me.

To Jane, you have such a sweet spirit, thank you for the precious moments.

...~*♡*~...

Introduction

I did not plan on writing a book; especially a book regarding the soul. I do not have all the answers. In fact, I have been wrong many times throughout my life. However, as I observe so many people in pain and suffering throughout the world, I feel compelled to open up my heart and share some of my beliefs and experiences with you, with the hope that it may help in some way. Please be aware that the contents of the book are my opinions and experiences. I encourage you to only receive what resonates with you. Sharing different beliefs and ideas opens the door to learn, heal, and grow together.

Throughout my life, I have been comfortable in the world of logic. Logic has been my rock. Since I was a young child, I pushed aside my intuition, including premonitions, even though they were accurate most of the time, because it was outside of my comfort zone. I am an attorney who represents abused and neglected children and I base my recommendations to the court strictly on evidence. To embrace intuition seemed contrary to common sense for so many years. It was only when I was faced with a moral dilemma that I realized I could no longer push my intuition aside in my personal life.

In 2006, Jason suggested that I write about my dreams at night. His suggestion took me by surprise because he was a skeptic like I have been for so many years. However, because so many of my premonitions and intuitive experiences were accurate, he believed in me and he wondered if my dreams at night were also premonitions. We joked about it and I put paper and a pen by my bed before I went to sleep. I woke up the next morning thinking I had not dreamed the night before, but I was wrong. I looked at the paper and saw some scribble, and it triggered my memory. I had dreamed about a young girl who had been abducted, and the details were startling and seemed real.

Despite my skepticism, I decided that morning to call into work and stay home for a few hours to search for the girl online. I decided at that moment that no matter what the cost, including losing my job, if I confirmed the girl was actually missing, I would call in the details to the authorities. I could not find her in the news as missing, and I was relieved. I thought it was just a dream, and I threw the paper away with the decision to never place a paper by my bed again. I was too busy with my family and work. Approximately one week later on the National news I saw a picture of the girl that had been abducted. I was saddened to realize she had been abused that entire time. My mind started racing. If I had only embraced my intuition years ago, I may have been more advanced, and been able to obtain details from the dream to help find the girl sooner.

Due to the fact I was too afraid over the years to step out of my comfort zone, I failed to help that young girl, and I thought about how many times I discarded my intuition, and about how many other people I could have helped. I made a promise to myself on that day that I would never allow my fears of intuition to guide my personal decisions as to whether or not to get involved. Every life is too precious and too important to allow fear to be the basis for decisions.

I am writing this book because intuitively I know it is meant to be written. I did not have the courage to start writing until now. It was in the midst of wanting to help someone who appeared overwhelmed with pain and grief, which prompted me to take initial action, and begin writing the introduction and first chapter years ago. *Love is more powerful than fear.* There are so many people in pain, and who feel lost, so if there is a message that I am meant to pass on, then I should be strong enough to relay the message regardless of the costs. I will be learning along with you as the book unfolds. I believe it is likely that there are those out there for whom this book is being written, and you will know who you are because the words will connect with you.

I am not going to mention different religions because divine love is seamless and overlaps most religions. Some of the major conflicts, and loss of life throughout history, have been caused by rigid focus on religious differences, which drains humanity from our world. It is meant for us to come together with a bond of mutual respect and appreciation for our different beliefs; meanwhile, developing connections to heal, not divide us. Sharing different beliefs with each other, with an empathetic heart, opens doors for growth instead of shrinking behind rigid walls. It is often in the midst of challenging each other that we learn the most and achieve the best outcomes.

It is my hope that some of the words will spark a light in you that will only continue to grow throughout your life. Please join me on the path to connect to our steady souls.

...~*♡*~...

A Love Letter from My Heart to Yours...

I have learned that I am filled with joy when I see people maximize their potential. As an introvert and private person at heart, I am now tearing down walls, and facing my fears to leap from my comfort zone with the hope that it may help others.

If a path in your life leaves you in a place where you feel lost and alone, may you follow your heart and intuition (the compass of your soul) until you feel at home. May you surround yourself with caring people who love you for who you are, heal with you, and when you are together bring out the best in each other. May you never allow others to define who you are, cause you to feel less than you are, or define personal success for you. On the contrary, may you connect to your steady soul, and gain the confidence to define your own life.

May you let the authentic colors of your heart illuminate, and may you feel the light within others. May you find ways to feed your steady soul, and feel peace, while contributing to the soul of the world. May you have the courage to choose love over hate. May you have the strength to stand up to injustice, especially for the most vulnerable. May you lead others through example, and not conform to the flow of indifference and toxicity. May you transform your anger into energy to effectuate positive change.

May you align your mind with your soul, and truly live, instead of continuing to grieve for your highest self. May you never let anyone shift you away from the infinite source of pure love and radiant light within your soul. May you force yourself to step out of your comfort zone, and may life embrace you back. May you reach out to the world from a source of kindness and love, which will create an immeasurable ripple effect of healing and peace. May you be healed and protected by divine love and colorful light.

It is a privilege to share this journey with you. Thank you for your precious time, and opening your heart. Please, take care.

Warmest wishes,

Leta B.

P.S. Remember, today is the beginning of your future, so be as creative as your heart desires in designing your life map...

Chapter 1

Your Steady Soul

Each one of us has a steady soul within just waiting to connect to the divine, a force greater than ourselves. *I believe our steady souls are unique divine signatures of pure love that existed before physical form, and will continue to exist after our physical containers are shed.* Meanwhile, the human side of us continues to flip in different directions to fill the void and the holes we perceive are within us. In the midst of chaos, often people overreact in an attempt to control their environment to offset the unsettling feeling of being out of control in their lives. It is often the impulsive immediate desire to feel better, or avoidance of pain, that leads us to make poor choices. The mind often has difficulty organizing all of the day-to-day input, which may create dysfunction. The drawing of a strong tree with the sun in the center within this book signifies a steady soul. The tornado underneath signifies the chaos that comes with life but also the clutter within our mind. The anger, anxiety, guilt, hopelessness, despair, and fears may paralyze and consume us if we allow them. At times, we are like trees without roots moving in all different directions, which is often toward perceived pleasure and away from pain. It is a delicate fine balance to align the mind and the soul, but that is how we reach our maximum potential. The cover of the book, with the picture of the sailboat, is a reminder of how there are times we need to adjust our sail to the wind to remain steady on our heart and soul paths.

People may try to patch the feeling of holes within many different ways; such as emotional eating, buying stuff, and/or using substances to numb the pain. Often we are running from one task to another or from one crisis to the next, feeling like there are no other options in our lives. Meanwhile, many of us make choices that starve our souls. The steady soul is secure, just waiting to be awakened and connected with the divine. In the midst of all the chatter in our minds, it is often difficult to hear the quiet divine whisper within us, guiding us in the right direction. To find the quiet inner voice, try to be self-aware as to what you are hearing, and what you are choosing to listen to. It takes practice to carve out the chatter from the divine inner voice. People may label this inner voice differently; such as conscience or the spirit. A leap of faith to flow with the quiet voice of the divine, especially when feeling vulnerable, may feel nearly impossible.

When we connect to the light within us, our loved ones, and to our life's true purpose, it brings true joy. *The soul is steady just waiting to be fed and to blossom.* The steady soul is full of love, peace, and compassion. The steady soul will stand up to injustice. The steady soul will strive for the highest good. The steady soul will lift spirits up instead of breaking other spirits down. The steady soul reacts from a place of pure love. The key is to make choices that fuel your soul.

Many feel the despair in their lives is too great to overcome. Some people will not engage in life because the layers of trauma or pain have suffocated the life out of them and they no longer feel any light within. I will share personal experiences only if I believe someone may benefit from the information. I have a desire to focus more on the light rather than the pain in this book; therefore, I will share only the amount I feel is necessary to be helpful to others. When I was a child, I felt very old and dead inside. I thought to myself, "If this is how life is then I do not care to be a part of the world." The level of abuse from my father nearly killed my spirit. I welcomed death, and prayed often that my life would be over. When I was approximately eight years old, I heard my mother talking about a family member, and how if he drank anymore alcohol that it would kill him. Now, as an adult, I understand that the statement was an extreme exaggeration; however, at that young age, I believed her and that night I drank as much vodka as I could consume. I felt so relieved that night because I thought I would be gone by the morning. I was very disappointed when I woke up.

Even in the midst of living in so much pain, I found some light. Everyone has their own spark of light, and the key is to find what ignites the light within you. I focused on changing what I could, which empowered me. I volunteered helping others at a nursing home and hospital, and teaching kids to swim. I also started working when I was eleven years old, and during my teen years spent as much time working as possible. I also enjoyed pouring my energy into caring for five of my nieces and nephews away from the home. I felt, at the time, that I could not safely change what was happening in my home except to stand up at times to my father in an attempt to protect my loved ones. Through helping others, I quickly realized that I enjoyed seeing people maximize their potential, and it made my spirit soar to see other people full of joy. As an adult, I realized that I could either allow the pain and anger to consume me, or I could decide to effectuate change by giving to others. I decided that I could not just live a carefree life, and ignore that families and children continue to live day-to-day in the midst of abuse. Therefore, as an adult, I chose a job to dive back into the mud in the hope of helping to provide a step stool so that families may choose to take the opportunity to pull themselves out of despair, and to live healthier lives.

Our steady souls are waiting for us to connect to the divine. We cannot change past mistakes and poor choices; however, today is the first day of the rest of our lives, and we can choose to begin truly living. We can define our own lives within circumstances beyond our control. We have the ability to allow the negative to just pass around us, and to refuse to take in the toxicity. Join me in creating a beautiful and healthy life today.

Chapter 1

Exercises

1. **A gift for your soul** – What activities, places, or people help replenish your soul? Decide how you may incorporate this list into your life.

2. **Connecting to the divine** – Find or create a quiet space that fills your soul. Use a meditative breathing technique that works for you. Meanwhile, clear your mind. If things pop into your mind, then picture mentally clearing them out. Use this time to center yourself for the day. Picture in your mind a bright light or colors, you choose, coming down and filling your body slowly. Ask that the divine remove all of the negative energy from your body and fill you with divine healing light and love. Visualize the negative leaving your body, and visualize your body filling with the divine light and love. Then visualize your loved ones, or people that could use your support, and ask that they be filled with healing divine love and light as well. Ask that the divine love and light surround, protect, and guide you and your loved ones throughout the day. I also extend my prayer to fill and surround the world with divine love and light.

3. **Managing the chaos** – In the midst of feeling out of control of your life, picture your favorite kind of tree. Picture the chaos in your life circling you like a tornado. Picture yourself as the strong tree in the middle with your roots extended into the ground. There is nothing that will make you sway; you will remain centered to the core of yourself. The courage to survive any storm you are facing in your life is within you.

4. **Defining your own life** – When you feel strong enough within to overcome painful memories, recall some of the most traumatic times in your life, only if you feel you can do this safely. Think about what you learned from the experiences. How can you transform these lessons into wisdom to improve your life and the lives of others? If it was someone else that caused pain or hurt, analyze your life and determine if the offender is still guiding your life today. You may not have the offender in your life, but if the anger or pain is still controlling your choices, then you have given power to the person who hurt you, and he/she is still in control, which often impacts your loved ones as well. Picture a rope connected to the memory or offender, and visualize cutting the rope and letting go. *Forgiveness is not condoning the behaviors of another person, but it is releasing the anger and hurt, so you may feel peace.*

NOTES

"My personal thoughts and feelings…"

NOTES

"My personal thoughts and feelings…"

...~*♡*~...

Chapter 2

Finding the Light Inside

It is a divine gift to find the light inside in the midst of despair. All of us have our trials and challenges in life; however, there are people who have experienced loss or obstacles so painful that they do not overcome them before leaving this world.

Please be aware that this chapter contains details of abuse and abusive language; please do not read this chapter if you feel it may affect you in a negative way. It was an extremely difficult decision to share such personal painful experiences with you, and share the moments that reflect my worst behaviors ever. However, I thought about all of the brave children in the child welfare system and other abuse survivors. If sharing some of my experiences helps others in some small way, then it is worth overcoming my fears of being open and vulnerable. There are people who have lived through much worse experiences, and I decided we cannot learn together if people pretend painful experiences do not exist, and are not willing to share. If you decide to read this chapter, I ask you to ponder what feeds the light within you because you are invaluable and worthy of truly living.

Our souls can connect to a divine force greater than ourselves, which contains infinite wisdom if we are open. First, I want to indicate that I share the following experiences as learning lessons, but I want to stress that I have forgiven my father, who passed away years ago, even though it was difficult. To me, forgiveness did not mean I condoned his behaviors, but I released the anger with the understanding that what I went through were learning experiences that gave me the tools to help others later in life.

As a young child, I would feel literally sick when my father would claim that the Aryan race is superior over other races. It makes sense to me now that I felt ill, because discrimination is poison. Discrimination has been a root cause of so many atrocities. In fact, when he made these toxic statements, I knew deep down they were lies. I would think to myself, "If this is how people are treated, then I do not want any part of this world." I knew within the core of my being there was no truth to it. How did I know that without any other input, at the time? How did I feel overwhelming kindness and love within me? Where did it come from? When he would talk negatively about homosexuals, I would also feel a weight within my body knowing that he was just being cruel. I would also feel ill when he would tell me women are to be seen and not heard, and women were created for men. *Every precious human being born should have the right to live, love, and maximize his or her potential without discrimination.*

There are times in our lives when it is difficult to feel the light within, and seems impossible to find even a glimmer. I was approximately six or seven years old, and my mother was visiting family out of town. I was in the bathroom, in pain and feeling dead inside, while filling the toilet with blood. I remember trying my hardest to cling to the toilet seat barely hanging on because I did not want to get any blood on the floor. I was more concerned about getting blood on the floor than the pain. Finally, I was too tired and weak to hold on, and fell to the floor. My father came in panicking, and yelling at me over and over again to stop bleeding. I am not sure what my father shoved in me to cause me to bleed because I just remember sharp pain, and trying to breathe, while he was pushing my face into the mattress. He stated numerous times that he had spoken to the hospital and was told if I do not stop bleeding I will die. Honestly, I do not think I cared about dying, just wanted to go to sleep and remain asleep forever. I felt dirty; like I was nothing. Logically, I know that I could not have stopped it from happening at that age but for many years, I still felt weak and ashamed.

Even though he caused the bleeding, for years he would tell the family at holiday dinners that I owed him my life because he saved me when I almost bled to death. Every time he made the statement, it reminded me that I did not belong in this world. I was not taken to the hospital, and realized years later that he probably did not even speak to the hospital. No one questioned his heroic story or, to my knowledge, asked what caused me to hemorrhage. It is an example of how much fear and control one person can have over other human beings, and the distorted thought process that develops with abuse.

My father quickly found out that his continual threats to get one of his guns, and kill me if I talked about what went on in the house, did not work against me. He was threatening a child who, while lying in bed, would count the posts and the top metal spokes on the canopy bed, praying to not have to live until eight years old. He quickly moved on to threatening how he would shoot family members in front of me, and then would shoot himself, but would leave me alive to feel the pain. He realized he could also manipulate me by kicking and beating our family dogs. He threatened Hell, stating the worst sin I could commit is talking about the family outside the home. He would detail how I would think that leaving the house would free me, and I could rest some day. Then he described the future, how I would believe he forgot about me, but he would show up, and kill my husband and children. He varied the scenarios for the future; for example, he would describe how easy it would be to light a match outside the house while my husband and children are sleeping. He would also describe how he would line up my husband and children, and would "blow their heads off", one by one, and would make me watch, leaving me alive to feel the pain. He reminded me on a regular basis, after the age of approximately eleven years old, when I stood up to him, that I was nothing but a f***ing bitch.

Blessings come in disguise sometimes. I am actually thankful he almost killed me when I was approximately six or seven years old because I believe it is likely that action scared him enough to stop him from years of blatant sexual abuse. He would require the doors to be unlocked throughout the house, and if any were locked, he would rage and punch the doors until they were unlocked. If he was able to see me dressing or in the shower, he would throw me a fifty dollar bill, which I just threw back knowing he was just hoping I would give in to him for money. My dear sister, eighteen years older than I, had to endure sexual abuse by him from five years old until thirteen years of age. I did not realize what she endured until I became an adult. She told me, after my mother passed away, that she informed my mother when I was three years old because she observed how he treated me, and it was a reminder of how she was treated when she was young. She informed me that he used the same threat to kill the entire family against her. However, with her, he also added that no one would believe her because she was just a dirty little girl.

My sister indicated, to protect me when I was three years old, that she went for a drive with our mother, and told her about the abuse from five years of age to thirteen years of age, and she described how our mother turned against her at that time. My father, over the years, repeatedly told me that my sister tried to kill me by trying to throw me through the plate glass window when I was three years old, and that is why she was told not to come back in the house. I believe my sister was trying to protect me, and it was courageous for her to speak up. If my sister's outcry had been heard, supported, and treatment obtained, then it may have guided the path of the future for my sister and family in a positive direction. My sister admitted to me that many choices in her life were made to commit a slow suicide because she did not feel worthy until the last years of her life when she recovered, and was finally happy. My sister passed away in October 2006 of a brain aneurysm. She looked like an angel the day she passed, and I believe it is likely she is watching over our family.

I developed coping skills while in survival mode. At times, even if I did not see my father walk into the room, I could feel the hairs on the back of my neck rise just from his presence, and would look around the room to see what household objects could be turned into a weapon if he began raging. When I was approximately eleven years old, he pushed me too far. I remember he was lying on the couch taking a nap, and I was standing in the hallway. He started laughing with a creepy tone. I asked him, "What is so funny?" He continued to laugh, and then he asked if I had ever butt f***ed. My mind immediately flipped to the incident I described when I was six or seven years old. I went into his bedroom and retrieved one of his hand guns, a .45 caliber semi-automatic. I put a clip in; however, I did not rack the slide to put a round in the chamber because I started thinking about how my mother would walk into the house and find blood all over. I am not proud of that moment, and it concerns me that I even had it in me to retrieve the gun to consider killing him. My action in that moment does not coincide with who I am, and it frightened me to feel that way.

My father knew my good friend in the house was my dog. He would beat and kick him when I would make him angry. Finally, he went too far, and my dog was bleeding internally to the point when I took him to the veterinarian, they had to put him to sleep. I could tell the veterinarian was wondering if I caused the injuries, but I just remained silent, and let him think what he wanted. I remember thinking that my dog was finally at peace. My favorite memories with my dog were the days when I came home from school and no one was home. I would get a big bowl of ice cream, and I would get him a snack, and we would sit and watch TV together.

My father had been a professional boxer when he was younger, and he was proud of his fighting ability. He reminded me that his fists were considered a weapon. He was smart enough with me, when he wanted to physically dominate me, to grab my neck under my hair, or grab the under hairs on the back of my neck to lift me up, and drag me around so he did not leave marks. I did not realize that I had a fractured neck until an x-ray I had as an adult due to ongoing neck pain. I do not know how the fracture in my neck occurred, and I do not know if he caused the fracture.

One day when I was sixteen years old, as I walked in the house to change uniforms for my second job, he was already escalated, and hit me in the side of the head as I walked in the front door. I fell to the ground. As he indicated that he was going to get the gun and blow my head off, I told him to go ahead but he better really do it this time because if he left me alive I would take him to Hell with me. I felt tired throughout my bones, and welcomed death. He must have felt it because he started backing up with a surprised look on his face. It seemed to startle him that I did not show any fear, or respond to the physical pain. For the first time, my mother came in, and started in on him about what he did. The conflict went down the hall into my room. He grabbed my mother and lifted up his arm to punch her, and I grabbed a glass figurine and slammed it on the dresser, and held the edge up in the air. I told him he should sleep with one eye open because I will slit his throat if he ever touched my mother or me again. He did not hurt her physically in my presence from that time on. After the incident, I went to work with a smile on my face, as usual. People may find that odd; however, when your daily existence includes suffering, then the emotional pain becomes almost routine. I truly felt, at the time, the only way I could stop him was to threaten him. I was wrong to handle it in that manner. It would have likely saved a lot of heartache for everyone, and increased the chance for treatment for all involved if I would have reported him to the authorities. In addition, it would have helped him receive the treatment he needed. My mother told me not to talk about what happened in the home. During the times he would become escalated, she would normally just ignore his behaviors and act vacant.

In regard to finding the light inside, during my teen years, it gave me hope for humanity to volunteer at the hospital, teach children to swim, and work at the nursing home. Working two jobs was a way to self-protect and escape; meanwhile, work gave me the ability to save enough money to move out of the house. Instead of allowing the sadness of watching my mother live in a painful marriage to consume me, I saved up money to take her to Hawaii while in my junior year of high school, and then treated her to Europe the year prior to her passing. I received such priceless gifts from watching her enjoy life while on vacation. Even though my mother seemed to have a smile and caring word for everyone she met outside of the home, she understandably appeared to feel like a shell of herself in the home. Spending time in the mountains and other natural locations also nourished my soul.

Finding the Light Inside

When I was seventeen years old, after high school graduation, I moved to California, and rented out a room in Irene's home. (Irene is noted in the acknowledgement section.) I was determined to be completely independent from anyone so that no one could hurt me again. Fortunately, I had sent two months worth of rent out to Irene to cover the costs in case I lost my money on the way out to California. My car did break down in the desert, and after the nearest mechanic in a small town asked how much money I had, he then told me how much the bill was, which was a good learning lesson for me. He did leave me enough money for gas and food to get me to California, which I appreciated. During the first couple of weeks, Irene must have thought I was boring because she would ask me to go out with her or eat with her, but I would decline each time. The truth was that I had to use the gas left over in the car to find a job, and I ate mainly noodles for a couple of weeks, until I found one. My plan at that time was to stay and work for a couple of months, and then move into an apartment while giving my mother an option to live in California if she wished to get out of her living situation, which she declined. However, Irene and I became so close that living there became home. Irene taught me that laughter, as long as it is not laughing at someone, is light and may have a healing effect. I would enjoy going to see comedies with her at the movie theater because her laugh is so contagious that it would spread to others in the theater. She has no filter and just says what comes to mind. I had no idea she suspected anything with my family until I walked into the room one day and she said, "Well, kid, you made it out alive." I was stunned, and it caught me so off guard that it penetrated the walls I had kept up for so many years. She was a neighbor when I was a young child, and I learned that she was likely one reason that my father wanted to leave California because she started to stand up to him about concerns she observed in the home. I began to open up some with her. Irene has a way, wherever she is, to get people talking. It comes natural to her, and I have observed out in the community that strangers tell her personal details of their lives. Irene is one of the strong willed Earth angels in my life. Irene is ninety years old and she has been such a blessing to me.

You never know when or how someone will make an impact in your life. I remember when I was eighteen years old and started working for a temporary agency. My first assignment was working for the City. The people working there were wonderful. I was allowed to work as hard as I wanted, and I was allowed to work in a variety of capacities. The position was supposed to be just temporary; however, after my supervisor was done interviewing for the full-time position, she came to me and stated she wanted to hire me full-time, and would work it out with the agency. The fact that a special person believed in me at such a young age, when everyone else working there were so much older, was life changing for me. I worked there until I received notice that my mother was terminally ill with cancer, and then I submitted my letter of resignation so I could return to care for her. I attempted to resign; however, my supervisor and the director/assistant city manager informed me they would not accept my resignation, and would hold a position for me no matter how long it takes. I am sure they did not realize what a precious gift that was to me. Honestly, after caring for my mother on and off for approximately a year, I was so drained of energy, I do not know what would have happened if I did not have a job to return to. Their act of kindness gave me hope.

The most sacred gift I gave my mother was not the trip to Hawaii or Europe, it was returning, while awake, to living with my father while caring for her. When I lived in the house before moving to California, I was in survival mode. To intentionally return to survival mode after coming alive was more difficult than I could have imagined. He would not physically hurt her with me there; however, the ongoing emotional damage was apparent.

While I was taking care of my mother, five of my nieces and nephews were dropped off for the night. I slept in front of the door to the downstairs where my nieces and nephews were sleeping. My father walked up in the middle of the night and asked me if I really thought I could protect them from him. I told him that I would kill him if he touched any of the children. He just laughed and walked off. I am not proud of myself and I should have handled the situation better.

My father was careful to contain the abuse in the home; however, he did mess up, and in the midst of rage, accidentally told my mother's doctor that he was going to shoot her in the head because she was in so much pain from the cancer. I got on the phone with the doctor and begged him not to call the police. I told him I am used to handling situations like this, and to let me deal with it. The doctor indicated I had thirty minutes to get my mother to the hospital, or he would call the police and have him put on a mental health hold. I did get her to the hospital, and the doctor had security keep my father away. My mother asked me to promise her that she would die at the house and not the hospital. I convinced the doctor to allow her to go home as long as there was a nurse in the home as well. I was wrong again to protect the dysfunction. I will have to live with the fact that I did not reach out to the authorities over the years as I should have.

One morning in 1987, I asked my mother why she became involved, and stayed in an abusive relationship with my father. It was just over a year prior to her death, on December 7, 1988. I did not realize at that time that my sister had already told her about the sexual abuse when I was three years old. I thought I had been protecting my mother all those years from knowing the truth. She explained that she felt she had the perfect childhood. She was raised on a dairy farm with her wonderful family, and she had never dreamed that people like my father existed. When she met my father, she was already emotionally in a weakened state from losing her first husband in a car accident. She stated my father was overly charming and sweet when she first met him. While they were dating, he would clean up her apartment, make meals, and pamper her. When her father was dying, she informed him that she would be leaving to spend time with her father before he passed. My father insisted on going with her. My mother did not want to return home and stay with a man if they were not married, because she knew it would upset her parents. She remembered thinking to herself, "This is either the nicest man in the world or he is evil." She married him just before going to see her father, and she stated it was like flipping a switch. He was a completely different person and he became jealous, controlling, and abusive. At the moment she knew she made a mistake, she saw rays of light coming through the clouds, and she thought to herself it will be okay, but that was not reality. My mother stated she did call the police while living in California on one occasion when he became violent; however, the officer, at the time, asked her what she did to make him upset, and told her not to do it again. She stated that my father threatened to kill her, and have his way with the children, or kill the children and leave her alive if she told others, or tried to leave him.

My mother still had the capacity to love her children and others; however, it was apparent she lost herself. My mother was giving by nature, and she was loved by the people who knew her. I share this story to help people avoid abusive relationships. I do not want to discourage you from committing to a relationship and depriving yourself of the joy that goes along with a real loving relationship. There are people that are genuinely kind, compassionate, and trustworthy. In my opinion, asking yourself if the other person brings out the best in you, and loves you for who you truly are, is a helpful guide. Also, it is enlightening to observe how they treat other people, and if their actions coincide with their words. The outward appearance of a person may be deceiving so it is important to listen to your own intuition. One of the most important choices in life is choosing who we should bring into our lives and into the lives of our children.

I understand that there are many people who live right now in environments where they do not feel physically and emotionally safe. People who, like our family, are protecting the dysfunction rather than facing the truth, and getting the family help. I urge every one of you who are living in an unsafe environment to reach out to safe trustworthy people and treatment providers to obtain help in a safe manner rather than allowing the pain to continue to cycle down through generations. I made the decision as a young adult to see a therapist to process and learn how not to allow the past to define my future. Furthermore, I have worked for over ten years on cases involving domestic violence and child abuse; however, I am not a treatment provider so I am not going to detail the potential short term and long term effects for you. I tried to raise examples of power and control through fear, and the distorted thought process that can surface in abusive situations. I also provided examples of what I did wrong.

Living with abuse can become a part of your routine just like brushing your teeth; however, that is an example of a distorted thought process. I knew a woman who would hide the knives before she went to bed at night, and she did not think anything about it because it was a part of her nightly routine. The dynamics of domestic violence and child abuse are complicated, so I recommend, if it applies to you, that you obtain information from experts in the field. Furthermore, mental health experts can help educate you on how trauma impacts the brain and the potential short term and long term emotional effects. It may be necessary to establish safe boundaries even with family. Every person and situation is different, so it is important that anyone who is suffering from abuse, and lives in constant fear of harm, tailor a safety plan and treatment that fits his or her situation to ensure the most favorable outcome.

It is an act of courage to speak out and it is not a betrayal, but an act of love because that is the only way you and the others involved can get the help necessary to change your lives for the better. While in the midst of the abuse, it is so difficult to see tomorrow, much less a brighter future. For those in the midst of living like this, I cannot stress enough the importance of working with an expert, and with people you can trust, to help design a safety plan. When victims attempt to individuate, it can be the most volatile time period. If you are in the United States and have credible evidence to suspect a child is being abused, there are child abuse crisis lines you may contact. Positive change can only occur with action. Your act of bravery may initiate a positive ripple effect in the life of an at-risk child. It may also prevent others from having to suffer the same experiences.

I feel strongly that it is important to not make assumptions by grouping people together. Every person is unique and has his or her own experiences. I cannot tell you how careful I was in making the decision to represent abused and neglected children. I promised myself that if I ever projected my past experiences, and made assumptions about a family I worked with because of my past, that I would cease representing abused and neglected children. I can promise you that I would have stopped working immediately. I repeatedly questioned myself prior to making recommendations and decisions, which is tiring, but it has made me a better attorney and advocate. I am so thankful that I have the ability to view every person as unique and different so I do not carry over assumptions from case to case or from my past to present. Working with families in crisis is serious and should not be treated lightly. If you are thinking about working in a field to help others because of your experiences, prior to making a final decision, I encourage you to first honestly ask yourself if there is a substantial risk you will project your past on to others, and determine if your past will be an asset or liability. There is a lot of wisdom to gain from life experience that cannot be fully understood through a book; however, transforming life events into wisdom is essential for progress and helping others.

During the most painful times, it is still important to appreciate the sacred moments. I remember when I was taking care of my mother when she was dying of cancer. We had discussions about her feelings of death and her fears for her loved ones. Even though they were difficult discussions, they were precious moments and were healing for both of us. I remember she wanted to pick out the dress for her own funeral. We went to the nearest department store and as we were looking through the dresses, a nice woman who worked for the store came up to help look for an outfit and asked, "What is the occasion?" My mother and I looked at each other not knowing how to respond, and then we laughed so hard that tears were streaming down our faces. Unfortunately, we could not stop laughing long enough to tell the store clerk before she walked away, probably thinking we were disrespectful.

I also remember my mother had difficulty when we went out in the community, in the later stages of her cancer, because of the looks people would give her. One time, she walked up to a friend so excited to see her, but her friend started backing up to get away from her with a strange look on her face since she did not recognize her. Once she realized it was my mother, she burst into tears because of how much my mother had deteriorated. *You find out who genuinely cares about you, and who your true friends are, during the most difficult times.* It hit my mother in the core of her being, and she asked me to promise to please curl the little bit of hair she had left due to the cancer treatment, the way she desired prior to the funeral. You should have seen me bring the curling iron into the funeral home and plug the curling iron in next to the casket before the public viewing. I am sure the staff had a good laugh when I left. I even smiled when I left because I knew wherever my mother was she was having a good laugh. *A promise is sacred.*

Physical death is something that everyone will experience, and there can be special moments during the grieving process. I spent the night sitting in the room with my sister who was still on artificial support only so they could conduct the surgeries for the organ donations in the morning. Even in the midst of sadness, it was still a time that I cherish because it was a chance to honor her life. My sister's co-worker arrived during the night with lovely flower lays, and we placed them on my sister, and spent hours talking about memories and celebrating her life. I highly recommend not allowing fears to keep you away from spending quality time with loved ones while they are sick or dying if they welcome the company. Sharing difficult times with loved ones is priceless and if missed cannot be replaced.

As an adult, I have fed the light within me in different ways. For some examples, I have not allowed my experiences as a child to define my future in a negative way. My spouse and I have poured our hearts and souls into raising four strong beautiful daughters. They are each unique and amazing human beings, and it has been a privilege for us to watch them grow up. We design our marriage the way we desire. I became an advocate for the best interests of abused and neglected children; meanwhile, utilizing what I learned to help others as well. I reach out to people with kindness and love in my heart to try to make a positive impact.

Some of the most treasured moments in my life have been working with children and families involved with the child welfare system, especially during the times they worked hard to achieve successful outcomes in their own lives. I learned so much from the many courageous children and from the parents as well. Many of the parents just modeled their parenting after the dysfunction of the family they were raised in. In regard to the parents who struggle with substance abuse, it is inspiring to watch the strength of some parents who are successful at breaking free from the network that supports their substance abuse, which sometimes includes setting boundaries with family and friends, and replanting themselves within a new support system. It is a gift to see when parents choose their children over drugs, abusers, and/or sex offenders. It is amazing to see the parents that successfully break the cycle of dysfunction, and decide to meet the needs of their children, which will likely cycle down throughout generations. It has also been an honor to observe when caring relatives, foster parents, and/or adoptive parents open their hearts and homes to abused and neglected children who cannot safely return home.

In January 2014, a hopeless feeling of despair led me to thoughts of ending my life. Considering those thoughts, along with my Multiple Sclerosis symptoms, I decided to take medical leave from the law firm. I am disappointed in myself because I know suicide injects poison into loved ones, and the psychological ripple effect is immeasurable for those left. I could list many reasons, but the real answer is I was wrong to allow my thoughts to get so negative. It is a scary bridge from being an attorney, appointed by the court on some cases, working strictly with logic, to disclosing private personal experiences and embracing my intuitive side. It is the hardest thing I have ever done because making the decision to transition the law firm, and take the leap into the unknown, has put a burden on my family, which I never wanted. I know it is difficult for loved ones to understand now; however, I believe it will be best for everyone later on. I have soul searched, and honestly I feel I can help more people at this time by facing my fears, and opening my heart to others who may relate to the struggle between logic and intuition. *The truth is that logic and intuition together are important for us to be whole. Striving to align our mind and soul is how we reach our highest potential.* I have owned and operated a law firm for approximately ten years, and I truly have an amazing team who pour their hearts and souls into serving our clients. If combining my intuition and logic is the best way I can serve humanity at this point, and contribute to the soul of the world, then I want to serve my purpose while I am here on Earth.

Feeling like you're successful can feed the light within you. Every person has his or her own definition of success. A person should feel free to define what success is for himself or herself, without judgment. I personally do not define success for myself by money, titles, or the illusion of power. I define success, for me, by loving and supporting loved ones through the difficult times, living an authentic life, and serving humanity.

In regard to finding the light within me, my heart soars when I see people maximize their potential, and truly live. I am grateful that what I enjoy most is seeing people full of joy. Also, nature is an artistic divine force that feeds my soul. *Transforming my anger into kindness has been my way to effectuate positive change.* Every person is unique and will need to find his or her own way to feed the light within.

Chapter 2

Exercises

1. **Despair** – When were the moments in your life that you felt the lowest and could not find the light within?

2. **Finding the light** – What feeds the light within you? How could you incorporate these things, steps, or people into your daily life?

3. **Support** – Who in your life brings out the best in you? Is there anyone in your life to break you down or hurt you? If so, what safe steps can you take to stop this from continuing? What steps can you take to receive the support you need?

4. **Spreading light** – In what ways could you extend the light within you to others?

5. **Honoring loved ones** – Every time you move forward in your life, or help others, you honor the lives of loved ones who have passed. What ways can you honor the lives of people who have passed on?

NOTES

"My personal thoughts and feelings…"

Finding the Light Inside

...~*♡*~...

NOTES

"My personal thoughts and feelings…"

...~*♡*~...

"It is a divine gift to find the light inside in the midst of despair."

...~*♡*~...

...~*♡*~...

Chapter 3

Transforming Pain and Hurt into Peace, and Receiving Blessings

Transforming pain and hurt into blessings is challenging, and can seem like a mountain too high to climb, but you do have the courage within you. Even though it is often extremely difficult to allow others to climb the mountain with you, it is important that we open up to safe and trustworthy people so that we are not alone in the journey. It is a gift to allow people into our hearts. If the layers of pain and trauma become so thick, we often close ourselves off to the world to eliminate the risk of being hurt again. It may feel more comforting to continue living in a self-made prison rather than risk tearing down the walls to only be hurt again. There are trustworthy people that will bring out the best in you; however, it often just takes practice to recognize who they are.

To transform hurt and pain into peace and blessings, it is important to determine what difficult lessons you learned from the experiences. The knowledge that you have now may be used to move your life forward, and to help others. There are times in our lives we are going to feel deep sadness and are not able to feel at peace. There are losses that are so painful that it is nearly impossible to comprehend continuing to live, much less creating something positive from the tragedy. However, in such cases, the tsunami of pain and guilt will not honor the precious lives lost. Punishing yourself time and time again will only cause more pain to you, and the people who love you. Every choice that is made to move forward in a positive way, to improve the world, and to help others, honors the lives of those lost. Furthermore, if the loss was caused by the intentional cruel acts of another person, allowing the ripple effect from the tragedy to destroy you, and those around you, only honors the offender. Everyone leaves this Earth at some time, and it is essential that we remind each other to cherish and honor the lives of our loved ones rather than focusing on the manner they left this world.

If you are hurt by someone, and you allow that pain and anger within you to pass on in the form of harming yourself, or someone else, then I believe you are honoring the very person who caused the suffering in the first place. Actually, I believe it is more than just honoring the person who hurt you, in some form, you allow the negative energy of that person to carry on through your actions. In addition, it opens the door for the offender to have power over you, and you may even give implied permission for the offender to guide your future without being aware of it. How many people are incarcerated because they allowed their anger from hurt to consume them, and the people who harmed them are out walking around moving forward with their lives? How many people self-medicate to the point their precious lives are destroyed from the aftermath of pain and hurt? How many offenders are still harming others even though they are deceased, because the pain inflicted on others while alive still infiltrates additional lives? This can even be applied throughout the world. There are some world leaders throughout history who committed horrific acts, and it is disturbing that in some form they live on through the minds and actions of others today.

In comparison, when you have felt real love and kindness from a genuine person, and you receive that kindness and love, while allowing it to live on through you, a greater force thrives. Furthermore, the energy of your loved one, in some form, lives on through your actions as well; meanwhile, you honor his or her life. I believe real love is the strongest force in existence. If you are hurt, or there is an injustice that has caused you or your loved ones to suffer, you can make the choice to allow it to take you down and feed the offender, or you can analyze the injustice and then choose ways to effectuate positive change. It may be that it does not have anything to do with the person or people who caused the injuries; it may be making a difference by helping society and others that creates a ripple effect of healing. No one can define you or diminish your character unless you give permission. When you continue to care about other human beings, and follow your heart and soul to live your best life, you take away the offenders ability to have power over you and to guide your decisions. I am grateful for world leaders who have passed away physically but their love for humanity and example still lives on through people today.

There are intentional acts of cruelty on a vast scale that are truly unthinkable for most human beings. There are times when a country or an international community is forced to take action to eliminate such atrocities by using force because there is no other reasonable alternative. The offenders need to be held accountable for their actions. However, in the aftermath of such tragedies, if the victims and loved ones allow their pain and anger to consume them and make choices to self-harm, or hurt others, then their actions honor the offenders rather than honoring the lives of the victims.

In contrast, if the resilient human spirit of the victims and the community rise up and make the choice to spread colorful light, kindness, and love to others, it will create an immeasurable ripple effect that honors the victims and their loved ones. Furthermore, it will minimize the chances of the toxic energy emitted by the offenders from carrying on.

To minimize injustice in our society, it is important to starve apathy. Lack of concern for human life adds to the layers of pain and hurt. When we remain silent while observing injustice, we miss opportunities to improve the future. I believe in some circumstances inaction can be a form of action. Anger may be transformed into energy to effectuate positive change. However, it is important to decide for yourself what or who you are willing to stand up for. By picking the battles in your life it is likely people will listen more when you speak up. When a person complains too much it can become merely background noise.

There are people and causes worth fighting for. Protesting in opposition to an injustice may be the best option in some circumstances. Using injustice as an excuse for violent protests raises the level of injustice; meanwhile, it will likely render them ineffective. In contrast, finding positive venues, to effectuate change, increases the chances for justice in the future while creating peaceful solutions.

If you respond to your hurt and pain by sharing kindness and love with others, it opens the door to feeling peace and blessings. Furthermore, since we are all connected, it will set an example for others, and may even help them find peace and be open to receive blessings as well. Meanwhile, you will be making a positive difference in your community and contributing to the soul of our world.

Chapter 3

Exercises

1. **Identifying the pain** – What are the memories, things, or people that are causing you pain? Do you feel you are suffering? If so, what are the reasons for your hurt? Do you feel you make decisions from the source of your pain at times? If so, has it impacted others?

2. **Transforming pain into kindness** – What are some safe acts of kindness towards others that you can incorporate into your life?

3. **Anger** – Do you feel anger has affected your health? If so, in what ways? Do you feel you pass on your anger to others? If so, in what ways? What steps can you take to turn your anger into energy to help yourself? How can you use the energy of your anger to make positive changes in society?

4. **Choosing love rather than fear** – In what areas in your life do you choose to let fear guide you rather than love? Have fears blocked out love in your life? How can you choose love over fear in the future?

5. **Peace and blessings** – Consider how you can maximize peace in your life while opening yourself up to feel blessings in your life.

6. **Support** – If you are not receiving treatment from a mental health provider, do you feel it would be beneficial to begin receiving formal treatment? If so, what steps can you take to receive the treatment? Who in your life is trustworthy and healthy to be a support?

NOTES

"My personal thoughts and feelings…"

NOTES

"My personal thoughts and feelings…"

...~*♡*~...

*"The character of society
coincides with how we treat
our most vulnerable members of society."*

...~*♡*~...

...~*♡*~...

Chapter 4

Awareness

Do you ever feel like overall as a society we are sleep walking sometimes? I do not know about you, but I feel I have been asleep at times in my life, merely surviving, or running from task to task, focusing on what I feel my responsibilities are without being truly awake. We are taught how to think from various sources from the time we are born. *We create opportunities for growth by questioning information that is fed to us, stepping out of our comfort zones, and by living with an open heart and mind.*

The threads of logic, intuition, and humanity should be beautifully interwoven through the fabric of our world. Throughout history, the level of awareness among individuals, society, and people around the world, has been evolving. In my opinion, the most important area for awareness in our world is humanity. If each one of us reached out with empathy and kindness in our heart to one person, there would not be a person that has not experienced compassion from another human being. The reality is there are people in this world who have never felt real love, empathy, or kindness. It is tragic that there are people who feel lost and completely alone in this world when there are billions of human beings on this Earth. In my opinion, one of the most disturbing kinds of stories in the news, is someone ill, injured, or dead in a public place while people just walk by and do not care enough to become involved. The lack of awareness and appreciation for other human beings injects pain into the core of my being.

The race for power and status, which are illusions, deflect our focus off of what is truly important. I have walked through many cemeteries, and I do not recall any tombstone that lists the title, income, and assets of the deceased. However, I have noticed the words "in loving memory" on many tombstones. Why does it take us so long to wake up? I do not understand why throughout history the masses have felt the need to lift themselves up by pushing other human beings down. Who decides who is valuable and who is not? Who has the right to define beauty for the masses? *When we minimize and disregard people for superficial and meaningless reasons, we drain the heart from civilization.* Every person is unique and makes a different impact in this world. I argue that it is the character, heart, and soul that create true worth. We make navigating this world so complicated and difficult for so many people. There are so many people that are not seen and valued. *The simple truth is that every human being should be born with basic human rights without suffering from discrimination.* There is no "but" at the end of the sentence, and there are no exceptions. It is that simple, yet we continue to make it so difficult for some to feel worthy of living. In a world of billions of people, I believe if you have even one person in your life you can fully trust, who will be there for you during the difficult times, and who loves you for who you are, then you are truly blessed.

Individual awareness

Today, does your life mirror what is in your heart and soul? As individuals, awareness of our strengths and weaknesses may assist with effectively navigating through life. Are you living life according to your authentic self? What do you pay most attention to in your life? Do you feel you live with an open heart or do you feel you have too many emotional walls up? Do you feel you are maximizing your potential? Have you surrounded yourself with people who love you and bring out the best in you? Are you living your life merely to please others? Do you embrace intuition and logic? Are you sensitive to energy? Do you see other people with your eyes, or feel their energies with your heart and soul, or both? Do you take time to notice when people around you are suffering and need assistance? No one can answer these questions for you. Furthermore, no one can define you unless you give your consent.

One of my weaknesses is that I often do not notice physical surroundings, which contributes to the fact that I am directionally challenged. However, I have come to realize that I am more sensitive when it involves intuition and energies, which is strength. As I discussed in the introduction, logic was my rock, and I would push aside my intuition because it was outside of my comfort zone, which I realize now was a weakness. I feared intuition. However, I have learned that intuition is an important sense that we should not deprive ourselves from being open to, or we limit our potential. Intuition is a part of me and I realize my life cannot coincide with my heart and soul fully unless I embrace it. I have forced myself to face my fears. *There is a vast existence beyond what our eyes can see, and if we close our minds we limit our possibilities.* Fears and anxiety can prevent us from living a life from the well of our soul.

Do the roles you fill in your life bring out the best in yourself and others? If you are employed, what is the vision at your workplace, and does it resonate with your soul? It does not need to be a big title or substantial income because jobs, regardless of the amount of pay, that contribute in a positive manner are important to the functioning of society. When we take pride in the quality of our work, in any position that assists others, we enhance our workplace and make a difference. If you are attending school, a part of a team, and/or belong to a group, the same questions can be answered. What does the soul of your school or team project? Does the vision resonate with your soul and do you, in the role you fill, bring out the best or worst in yourself and others? I have observed how a few negative attitudes can permeate throughout, and lower the character of the workplace, school, and/or team. In comparison, strong people who truly care can often guide in a positive direction and raise the level of character and quality work. In my opinion, it is possible to teach someone policies and procedures but the heart, soul, and character of a person are what truly matters.

As an individual, in what ways do you contribute to society? Even one act of kindness makes a difference in the world as we are all connected. When we come in contact with another person, we do not know all of the trials or losses he or she is struggling with from day-to-day. Also, we do not know just how much a kind gesture towards another person may impact his or her life. I have heard you need to help yourself before you help others. It is easier and takes less energy to give to others when feeling at your best; meanwhile, giving while you are feeling down takes more strength and character. People are not perfect, and it is our imperfections that help make up the complexity of us. Every person is unique, and everyone has something to contribute if he or she chooses to do so. If we wait to assist and give to others until we feel our lives are perfect, then we will miss so many opportunities to make a positive difference. It may be that another person may be more open to us because of our imperfections. You may find your authentic self through service. Have you ever considered what impact you have made in the lives of others, and why the world is a better place because you lived?

Societal awareness

In the interest of bringing people together with a foundation of mutual respect, I will not focus on this area in too much detail. Every society has its own culture, traditions, and laws; therefore, it is important not to make assumptions in general. In addition, every society has its strengths and weaknesses. Therefore, I will simply raise some questions for you to ask yourself so you may apply them to the location you reside. What does the character of your society and government as a whole communicate? Do the laws bring out the best or the worst in the people? Are all human beings valued in your society? How does your society treat the most vulnerable members? What within your society divides people? What within your society brings people together? What do you feel are the strengths and weaknesses in your society? What does the soul of your society project? Does the society as a whole resonate with your heart and soul?

World awareness

All of us on this planet are a part of the human family. When we make assumptions about an entire country based on the government or the actions of some, we miss the richness of all of the unique precious lives that are the heart of the country. In the news, we hear about people around the world, and it is important to remind ourselves that they feel, have dreams, and have loved ones just like almost everyone else. What does the heart and soul of your country project out into the world? What would you like to see the soul of the world project?

Chapter 4

Exercises

1. **Awaken** – Is there some area in your life you wish you were more aware of and would like to awaken within you?

2. **Beyond the tangible** – Do you feel you focus more on the physical in the world, or are you more sensitive to energies? In connecting with others, do you see people more with your eyes, or do you feel their energy?

3. **Vulnerable members of society** – Do you notice when people are having difficulties or struggling? If so, describe a situation that you reached out to someone in need. What were the results? Is there a way you would handle it in the future?

4. **Societal changes** – What would you like society to be more aware of? What changes would you like to see? Is there anything you can do to make the changes?

5. **Soul of the world** – What would you like the world as a whole to be more aware of? What changes would you like to see? In what ways can you make a difference?

Awareness

...~*♡*~...

NOTES

"My personal thoughts and feelings…"

Awareness

...~*♡*~...

NOTES

"My personal thoughts and feelings…"

...~*♡*~...

*"Until you align your mind with your soul,
you will continue to grieve
for your highest self."*

...~*♡*~...

Chapter 5

Aligning Mind and Soul

Aligning the mind with the soul may be difficult, especially when we are receiving input from all different sources on a daily basis. Society appears, at times, to flow against the grain of our highest selves, which may interfere with our minds coinciding with our souls. How do you define the soul? People have different definitions and labels to describe the soul. *I believe our steady souls are unique divine signatures of pure love that existed before physical form, and will continue to exist after our physical bodies are shed.* Meanwhile, our individual souls are part of an abundant divine life source, which if our connections are open, nourishes the soul. *Divine love is the strongest force that exists, and is the seed to create miracles. Divine love is the thriving thread that connects us all.* Our egos may interfere with our soul connecting to the divine. Human emotions such as fear, pain, and insecurities often cloud clarity of thought. Our logical minds may not be open to divine information because it does not coincide with societal norms. Some people may not want to adhere to the flow of his or her steady soul because the road may feel too difficult to follow; however, it is how we fulfill our true purpose in this world.

Today, as I write with the knowledge, I have lost a solid connection with my steady soul, and I am in the midst of overwhelming sadness. I wonder if I should write this book when I am at the lowest time in my adult life. It is a reminder that in our lives there will be times we feel lost, and need to steady ourselves. We have the free will to give up on life, or to move forward. In my opinion, when in pain, it feels easier at times to let go of life rather than overcome this difficult, and sometimes almost unbearable life obstacle course. Unfortunately, when we are in pain and suffering, it hurts our loved ones as well. Today, I choose to open my heart to divine love, and accept the challenges in life. I hope you will choose life, and open your heart along with me. As I write, at times with tears in my eyes, we are sharing this journey together as we are all connected.

To align our minds with our souls, we need to listen to our inner voice that guides us in the direction that illuminates the best within us. Ironically, when we are trying to listen to our inner voice, it is often when we feel the greatest pull from our ego to travel in a negative direction. To sort out the inner voice from the ego chatter, ask yourself what brings out the very best in you? Who brings out the best within you? When do you feel you are striving for your highest good? Do the choices you make mirror your heart and soul? Do you live a life just to please others? Do you avoid truly living because you are afraid of leaving your comfort zone? Do you live a life reflecting your authentic self? What feeds your soul and reinforces your positive thoughts? These are personal questions for each one of us as we are all unique with our own strengths and weaknesses. Answering these questions will help guide each one of us to make decisions that coincide with our steady souls.

The environment we subject ourselves to may infuse life, or drain our very being. Peer influence can be such a toxic contagious force, if accepted. We are all connected, and as individuals, we either contribute, or take away from the soul of our world. When people group together, they can combine efforts to illuminate humanity, or to breakdown the character of our society. When groups use their bond to break others down, I personally refer to this as the group mentality. When I refer to the group mentality, I mean that the individual conscious and moral character becomes drowned out by the toxic noise of the group. In my opinion, the group mentality can be dangerous. The group mentality may be present in our daily lives, whether subtle or blatant, it can interfere with aligning mind and soul. It is easier to break someone down than taking the time and energy to build them up. Unfortunately, the group mentality arises at times in all areas of our society; such as the work place, school, politics, religion, social media, and even in some families. As you reflect on your life, how often have you heard a group using words or actions to break others down, and even though you did not agree with it, maybe even felt sick inside about it, still allowed others to believe you feel the same way? It takes courage to speak from your heart, especially when it increases your vulnerability, and may irritate or anger other people. If it is a case of bullying, it may be that you choose to be silent rather than putting yourself at risk to be subjected to the aggression or violence. *When we do not honor the core being of who we are, I believe it can affect our emotional, spiritual, and physical health.*

To remain steady within chaos is difficult. Is the mind and soul of the area you work in aligned? I will share an example of the field I work in; meanwhile, you may apply it to your work and circumstances, if you desire. While working as an attorney for the best interest of abused and neglected children in the child welfare system over the past ten years, I did feel that my mind coincided with my soul, at the time. I worked with some amazing hard working people who care deeply for the welfare of the children. However, I also became disheartened to observe the indifference and lack of concern in some people and organizations. There are too many children dying from non-accidental deaths and neglect. I am so thankful none of the children on my cases passed away. Children are precious, and we need to invest the time and care to ensure their needs are met. Children should not feel like a number. *I remember thinking to myself, "I understand everyone is different, and it is a personal decision to genuinely care about other human beings; however, if someone does not care about others, at least obtain employment where you do not impact our most vulnerable population."*

The character of our society coincides with how we treat the most vulnerable members of our society. The children within the welfare system deserve to feel important, safe, and to experience a childhood just as any other child. The heart and soul of the child welfare system is the children and their families. Politics, money, and corruption should not guide people or organizations involved in the child welfare system. Fortunately, in the judicial district I worked in, we were privileged to have some exceptional judicial officers and staff who truly cared about the best interests of the children, and some wonderful attorneys. In addition, the Court Appointed Special Advocates program, ("CASA"), a non-profit organization, is a wonderful support for children in the system. A CASA is a volunteer child advocate who provides a voice for the child. I believe if every child in the child welfare system was assigned a CASA then more lives would be saved.

To align the mind and the soul of the child welfare system, it is essential that decisions and recommendations are based on the protection of the children. In the child welfare system, one non-accidental death is one too many in my opinion. In some locations, there have been efforts to keep child abuse and neglect cases out of the court system. If sufficient support is tailored to meet the specific needs of the family, in order to effectively ensure the safety concerns are addressed within the home, then that is fine. However, it is important to be aware that in those cases the children do not receive the added protection from the court, CASA, and attorney, which also offers checks and balances to minimize the chances for abuse of power. Professionals involved in the child welfare system have the ability to collaborate to develop and implement creative plans to ensure a solid safety net for the children is in place. For one example, I read a news article, years ago, about a child who was involved in the child welfare system, who died from starvation and dehydration, even though the school had reported concerns to child protective services. Due to the news article, our office started sending out school feedback forms for school aged children to increase the chances that teachers would notify our office directly if concerns arose with the children we represented. The feedback forms have been invaluable to help ensure the wellbeing of the children, and have created more of an ongoing rapport with the schools. Another example, it is possible to develop a plan to locate runaways who are involved with the child welfare system to minimize the risk that they fall victim to human trafficking, drugs, or other harm. The creative planning is endless to improve the child welfare system with people who truly care and are invested in the children and families.

Families in dependency and neglect cases are encouraged to disclose and address dysfunction rather than protect it, and it is important that the same is expected from the professionals. Some children involved in the child welfare system have never thought about what they want to be when they grow up because they have merely survived day-to-day. When the basic needs of children are met, and they feel emotionally and physically safe, then they can focus on progressing in their own lives; meanwhile, minimizing the chances of the dysfunction cycling down to future generations. The children should receive the treatment necessary to learn from their experiences, and be encouraged to transform their anger into wisdom and motivation, to change their lives for the better. I treasured the moments when children and families reached their potential and had successful outcomes. In cases, where the children cannot return home, then the alternative caretakers who care enough to open their hearts and homes; such as relatives, foster parents, and/or adoptive parents need to receive sufficient support to meet the needs of the children in their care. If children are adopted, then the adoptive parents should receive the services and support necessary to maximize the chances for successful adoptions. Every child deserves a safe and loving forever family.

I did raise concerns about some of the problems I observed in the child welfare system. I received notice that our law firm could not accept new cases to represent children in the system, in the future, after our current case loads were completed. Our team was devastated, and our hearts broken, because we care so much about the children. However, I would have still raised concerns even if I could go back in time because, if I did not, then I would have been going against my heart and soul while contributing to the problems in the system. I am confident that our team members, who have such beautiful hearts, will continue to make a difference in this world.

In your life, how do you feel you can align your mind with your soul? Today, I am trying to align my mind with my heart and soul. My wish for my daughters has been that they would develop with the tools and skills to handle almost any situation with confidence in themselves. They are all four mature, courageous, and kind young women, and they make positive choices in their lives. They are making a difference in this world. I believe in them and their ability to successfully accomplish any goals they are willing to work hard to achieve. My wonderful spouse has been successful in achieving his career goals, and he is now starting hobbies since the girls are spreading their wings. At this moment, aligning my mind with my heart and soul, I want to donate so that a precious heart may receive the transplant necessary to truly live. Then it is my wish that we will be able to serve humanity in a variety of capacities. I am writing this book with the hope that opening my heart and sharing experiences will help others.

All of us have the choice whether to fulfill our purpose. We may be guided in various directions to serve. I believe we can have many different callings, and we do not have to put ourselves into a strict category to navigate this life. Furthermore, accepting and assigning labels to define us may create walls rather than doors. If we do stifle ourselves in a rigid manner, we ignore the complexity of our core being, and will likely miss many opportunities to serve. I have learned that one area of my life that I stifled is creativity. I am inspired by people who have allowed their artistic creativity to blossom and thrive. Our world is a richer place because of the people who have the confidence to share their artistic gifts and fulfill their artistic life purpose. Do you feel your mind and soul are aligned, and are you fulfilling your life purpose? If not, if you aligned your mind and soul today, how would that impact your life and the lives of your loved ones?

As I provided the example of the child welfare system, we can apply aligning mind and soul to all areas; such as family, employers, organizations, churches, towns, governments, countries, and the world. All living things make up the heart and soul of our world. If world leaders made decisions aligned with the soul of the world, it would not only raise the vibration of the world we live in, it would maximize our potential as a human race. If decisions made around the world granted everyone basic human rights, which would include living free from discrimination, we would finally acknowledge the true value of human life.

Chapter 5

Exercises

1. **Aligning your mind with your soul** – In your life, do you feel your mind is aligned with your soul? If so, in what ways? If not, what steps do you feel you could take to align your mind with your soul?

2. **Love is stronger than fear** – Do you feel your life mirrors what is in your heart and soul? In what ways? If not, what steps can you take to modify your life to coincide with your heart and soul? Do you have fears about living an authentic life and still being accepted? If yes, what can you do to overcome your fears?

3. **Together, making a positive difference** – Reflect on groups of people that have come together and have made positive differences in the world.

4. **Group mentality** – Reflect on times in your life where you have noticed the group mentality having a negative effect. Write down situations in which you wish you would have spoken up, but did not. Write down the reasons you feel you did not speak up. Do you want to speak up if a similar situation arises? If so, write down

how you would handle the situation differently in the future.

5. **Standing up for what you believe** – Each of us decides in what circumstances we are willing to stand up for what we believe in. List some situations you have spoken up. How do you plan to handle these situations in the future?

6. **Aligning mind and soul** – Do you have any thoughts and suggestions about aligning mind and soul for companies, societies, and the world?

7. **Map your future** – Design a creative map, which aligns your mind and soul, for your future.

NOTES

"My personal thoughts and feelings…"

NOTES

"My personal thoughts and feelings…"

Chapter 6

What You Feed Will Grow

What we feed will grow individually, among society, and throughout the world. If we feed fear, anxiety, hate, indifference, and prejudice, it will infiltrate our veins while limiting our potential. Feeding kindness, empathy, love, and compassion heals and cures.

Fears

Life is already difficult. If we feed the fears within us then we throw additional obstacles in our path. If we face our fears, it may allow us to achieve goals. For one example, I remember when I was nine months pregnant with my youngest daughter, and decided to apply to law school because I wanted to give back by being a child advocate for abused and neglected children. I had a lot of fears. How could I possibly attend law school at night while taking care of four daughters, three years old and under? For those of you good at math, my oldest daughters are twins. I questioned if I was smart enough. I knew that I could not just tell the girls they could do anything, I had to show them it is possible, so I faced my fears. My spouse was so supportive. I would take care of the girls during the day, and in the evening, he would care for the girls. I could have fed my fears by buying into the psychological stress of law school, but instead, I decided to wake up each morning at 4:00 am, and I would only study until the girls woke up. I learned how to effectively study in short periods of time out of necessity. If I did not overcome my fears and self-doubt, I would have missed over ten years of working with precious families in crisis.

Societal Labels

Human beings with disabilities or illnesses are more than just a label. There are countless people who suffer daily from disabilities or illnesses. If we focus only on the condition, and not resilience of the human spirit, then we tend to define and see people only for their limitations. There are countless people who suffer from medical, mental health, or substance abuse conditions that substantially impact their quality of lives.

There are conditions beyond our control; however, how we respond to them within our limited capabilities is within our control. I had stomach ulcers as a child, and as an adult, I live with relapsing and remitting Multiple Sclerosis symptoms. I believe emotional stress, and living in a toxic environment, can have a substantial impact on health. Overall, I am in good health; however, there are people with debilitating conditions that make it nearly impossible to function on their own. The more people are seen as human beings rather than labeled by the disease, or condition itself, it will encourage them to shine in the midst of challenges.

Choice to build people up or break people down

Every day we can choose to build people up or break people down. It takes more strength and care to build people up. Bullying infects our communities with pain and violence, which is contagious, and weakens the fiber of humanity. In my opinion, using some words, especially cruel weighted words, may feel more violent than fists. People who bully others have allowed their fears and weaknesses to overwhelm them, so they reach out in desperation to knock people down in an attempt to pull themselves up. It takes courage to embrace emotions. People who bully, often fear emotions while feeling chaos and lack of control inside, which feeds anger. Instead of being strong enough to transform their anger into kindness and positive change, to obtain a sense of self control and power, they often take their anger and emotions out through other people. In addition, people who bully others may be fearful of being different, and leaving their comfort zone, so they attack people who are brave enough to be themselves.

People who bully may have been bullied themselves and are just carrying on the cycle by modeling the same behaviors. Bullies may be an individual, group, or a country. Some people have the misperception that bullying reflects strength, and may decide to align with the perceived power; however, in actuality, they are merely feeding weakness within themselves. When people spew hurtful words, or make fun of other people, it reflects like a mirror on the person spewing the toxins, it is not a reflection of the other person. When peers remain silent while observing bullying behaviors, they drain character and contribute to spreading the infection. Furthermore, bullying may have long lasting effects throughout the life of the victim and the bully. *No one has the ability to define who you are unless you give permission.* It takes vigilance and strength of the human spirit to eliminate bullying as it surfaces individually, as a community and as a world family. I believe the death of the human spirit is much more devastating than physical death. It takes courage to choose love, empathy, and kindness over hate.

Character of Society

In our community, what we focus our energy on will become our priorities. If we pour our energy into magnifying our differences, then we will be divided, and stagnate. However, if we pour our energy into mutual respect and appreciation for our differences, then we will come together and become unstoppable. Focusing on the superficial; such as gossip, things, and drama will breed superficial outcomes. If as a society we place more value on people for their physical appearance; such as weight, skin, eye color, and height, versus their heart and character, then we are draining the wealth and heart out of our society. Meanwhile, we deprive our society of a unique rich blend of human contributions. The true wealth of society is the depth of love, empathy, and compassion for each other as human beings. We have the ability to value the complexity of each individual and his or her contribution to humanity. If we focus our energy as a society on substance; such as humanity, education, and mutual respect for our differences, then as a society people will be lifted up, and we will maximize our potential. In comparison, if society tolerates bullying, violence, and prejudice, then the character of society becomes ill and broken.

Connections

We are all connected and the energy we emit impacts others. Every person we come in contact with, we impact in a positive or negative way whether it be slight or substantial. I believe there are some people who get out their emotions through others without even being aware they are doing it. Emotions make some people uncomfortable. Depending on the level of impact, our emotions may affect a person to the point that it guides his or her future behaviors.

The following is a hypothetical example of just a brief encounter: You are having a frustrating day, which makes you angry. You drop by the grocery store to pick-up a few groceries. At the checkout counter, the customer service representative feels your anger and frustration. You will not know if you influenced him enough to guide how he treats customers after you leave. It may be that your frustration and anger is passed on to other customers as well as people they connect to later on. It may be your anger causes him anxiety, and ruins the rest of his day. When he goes home, you do not know if he will still be carrying your anger and frustration to the point it affects his family. In contrast, instead of passing on your anger and frustration, when the customer service representative asks you how you are doing, you are empathetic and make the effort to connect to him in a positive manner. You may even joke around with him to create some smiles and laughter between the two of you. The representative is lifted up by your encounter. You, giving of yourself in those few moments, even though you were having a difficult day, may inspire him to carry on the positive energy to future customers, and may even travel home to his family. The example I provided is a hypothetical of a brief encounter. Can you imagine the impact we could have on someone we have a substantial encounter with? How we treat other people matters.

I will share an experience that impacted me to my core. I was at a funeral and it just happened to take place at the same funeral home I saw my father's body at, years prior. I did not anticipate when I sat down that I would feel an overwhelming feeling of my father's energy since I had not felt it at all since he passed. I had this overwhelming feeling of suffocating despair. A kind person sat down in the same pew as me, and all of a sudden I felt this wave of kindness and light, and the negative dissipated immediately. It was a beautiful experience. I wish that healing wave could be spread to all.

Prejudice

Prejudice still exists today and is poison in the veins of our world. At some point in history, people had the destructive thoughts and delusions that one skin color, race, gender, or physical feature is superior to another. The delusions spread like a disease involving entire groups believing they are superior. These destructive thought patterns have lasted throughout generations, inflicting pain and suffering beyond comprehension. The level of cruelty shown to some homosexuals and transgendered people is tragic as well. Human beings should be born with equal human rights, living free from discrimination. The world would have been saved from the ongoing pain, suffering, and prejudice if discrimination had been eliminated prior to infiltrating perceptions around the world.

Love

Love is so powerful it is difficult to define in words. *Love is the true essence of life.* I believe that to truly live, it is essential to experience real love. It takes courage to open your heart; however, there are trustworthy people who are definitely worth the risk of being hurt. Deciding who to open your heart to is difficult. In deciding who to trust, I try to assess if a person is genuine. I observe to see if words coincide with actions, and if the person treats other human beings with respect and kindness. I try to follow my heart and intuition. The amount of time we have on this Earth is uncertain. When we fail to tell the people we care deeply about how much they mean to us, then we cheat the people we love. It is tragic, but understandable, when people go through life too fearful to love. Often, people who truly love us will bring out the best in us. If we allow ourselves to be open to connect to divine love, then it will increase our capacity to love others. I believe genuine love creates an immeasurable healing effect on people, society, and the world.

Chapter 6

Exercises

1. **Individual: feeding strengths and starving weaknesses** – What ways do you feed your strengths? What ways do you feed your weaknesses? What strengths would you like to feed in the future? What weaknesses would you like to starve in the future?

2. **Societal strengths and weaknesses** – What weaknesses do we feed as a society? What ways can we feed our strengths as a society?

3. **Courage to choose love over hate** – How do you feel we can feed kindness, empathy, and love, rather than hate in the world? How do you feel you can help?

4. **Authenticity** – Do you feel you have allowed others to define you? If so, when and how? How could you ensure no one but you defines yourself in the future? Do you feel some members of society are unfairly labeled? If so, in what ways? What steps can you take to see people for themselves rather than labels?

5. **Prejudice** – In what ways do you believe we could help to eliminate discrimination? What

steps can we take to evolve around the world so that every human being is born with basic human rights? What steps can be taken to develop mutual respect for our differences?

6. **Bullying** – Have you participated in bullying or observed bullying? What did you do? Is there something you would do differently in the future? What steps can be taken individually and collectively to eliminate bullying?

...~*♡*~...

NOTES

"My personal thoughts and feelings…"

...~*♡*~...

NOTES

"My personal thoughts and feelings…"

"Children will often rise or fall according to the expectations of loved ones in their lives."

Chapter 7

Children Are Blessings Not Burdens

Children are blessings not burdens in our families, our society, and in our world. I believe children can feel if their caretakers view them as burdens or blessings, and it can have long lasting effects. Children may rise or fall to the expectations of important people in their lives. If children have a foundation; such as love, safety, and confidence, it increases the chance they can launch from that point to maximize their potential. It is essential that children learn how to weigh pros and cons to make decisions. If children do not develop skills to have self-discipline within them to make safe choices, then outside authority; such as caretakers, teachers, and possibly even the criminal justice system, will have to provide discipline, which may carry into adult years.

It helped with our daughters to let them know that they have a choice to either develop the self-discipline within themselves or we will be forced to make decisions for them. They were told that if they are making positive choices and being responsible, then they have a lot more freedom to make their own decisions. However, if their actions reflect that they cannot make positive safe choices for themselves, then decisions will be made for them, and their lives will be much more narrow and structured. Fortunately, they are four responsible young women who make positive choices in their own lives. There are no perfect parents, we all make mistakes in parenting at times. Children often model behaviors of caretakers. However, if the children have the self-esteem and an internal moral compass, then it increases their chances of moving forward despite parenting failures.

If children learn empathy and compassion for other human beings when they are young, it will positively impact their lives as well as the people around them; meanwhile contributing to the soul of our world. I wish our education system would have a life skills section that starts in kindergarten and follows all the way up through high school, teaching how to weigh pros and cons to make safe decisions in their lives, having empathy for all human beings, and teaching other important life topics. The reality is there are many children who are not taught how to make safe positive choices and to treat others with kindness by their caretakers, and it impacts our society in many areas.

There are children who have special needs and may not have the ability to develop the self-discipline to function on their own in life. Therefore, that is when society should tailor services and support to give them the opportunity to maximize their potential. *The character of a society coincides with how we treat the most vulnerable members of our society.* I have a niece who has been diagnosed with autism, and our family has learned so much from her. She is such a blessing in our lives and she brings out the best in all of us. Just because a person suffers from a disability does not mean that he or she is less of a human being. Furthermore, it may be the disability magnifies the strengths in a person while reminding all of us about what is truly important in life. In circumstances where we can prevent children from having to suffer from disabilities, as a society, we should take the steps to minimize the effects. For one example, fetal alcohol spectrum disorders ("FASD") is the leading preventable cause of mental retardation. To minimize the number of children forced to suffer throughout his or her life from fetal alcohol spectrum disorder would require educating mothers to not drink alcohol while pregnant or during a period they believe they may become pregnant. However, many people are not even aware of the effects of drinking alcohol while pregnant, and many of the children suffering from the disorder do not get their needs met. Furthermore, it often limits the ability of understanding cause and effect, and some become lost in the criminal justice system.

When children are exhibiting negative behaviors on a regular basis, we need to try to understand the core of what is truly causing the problems so that they can get the support they need before it defines their future, and has a negative impact on others. We also should separate the behaviors from the core of the children themselves. Over the past ten years of representing abused and neglected children, I noticed that some of the children who initially displayed the worst behaviors and anger turned out to be the strongest and kindest inside because a lot of their anger stemmed from caring so much, and they felt the injustices so deeply. I found it interesting when some people would list off the behaviors of children in the child welfare system as if they had no idea why they were displaying certain behaviors. I would sometimes raise the question, "Why would we not see these behaviors with what the child experienced?" Our children deserve more than to quickly label them, and leap to prescribing medications prior to exploring other ways for them to heal and gain the skills necessary to maximize their potential. Labels and diagnosis provide structure and consistency in mental health treatment, which is important. However, it is also essential to ensure that people are not seen as labels or files but seen as precious human beings with the ability to progress most of the time. It is also critical as a society we do not allow money associated with pharmaceuticals to guide. If someone is deemed as a lost cause then it is likely the person will prove the cynics right. I do not believe we can underestimate the healing that can come from genuine caring, and taking the time to understand others rather than leaping to assumptions. It warms my heart when I see people who genuinely care about human beings more than their titles or income. I feel joy when I see people overcome obstacles in their lives and thrive.

I shared the moments with you in my life when I displayed my worst behaviors because I am being completely open so that we can learn together. *For example, if I had killed my father, I do not believe I would have told about the abuse because, at the time, I had the distorted perception that it would have been a betrayal to the family, and I would have likely just pled guilty.* The reality is speaking out, and getting help for the family would have been what was best for the family. Who knows how long I would have spent incarcerated. My four daughters may not have been born. The ripple effect of our actions is real and can be positive or devastating. How many children are enduring abuse from someone in their lives and are acting out to protect themselves, but are merely deemed as problem children? How many of those children grow into adults and enter the criminal justice system? Honestly, overall, in most areas, except when I was standing up to my father, I was mature, kind, and responsible as a child. I worked two jobs, went to school, and volunteered to help people. My mother did not understand why I did not go out and have more fun with the other kids. However, what if my poor behavior was not just towards my father in moments I felt it was necessary for me to protect? What if I allowed what was going on at home to affect my behaviors at school, work, or led me to choose substances to numb the pain?

I want to be careful to stress that just because children are displaying negative behaviors, it does not mean that the parents' actions are the root cause of the behaviors. Children, just like adults, need to accept accountability for their own actions. There may be many reasons a child is displaying negative behaviors, and guilt goes against the grain of moving forward. All of us make mistakes and all of us have areas where we can improve. We need solutions and not to search for blame.

Education is a doorway for children to maximize their potential. It is important that children are safe while attending school. As a society, we need to ensure that our schools are a safe haven for our kids. It is imperative that children learn how to have empathy for other people, starting in preschool. I have heard people say that it is a job for the parents not the school. However, there are many children who do not have caregivers who are willing or have the ability to teach kindness and empathy for other human beings. There are children who feel lost, worthless, and alone. As a community, we can be as creative as we desire in helping to develop a foundation for our children. Is there a more important basic curriculum for our children and our society than teaching children how to make safe choices, and have mutual respect for other people? The effects of bullying are immeasurable and often long term. If children view other people as human beings with feelings and worthiness instead of objects or numbers, it would likely increase safety in schools. If children, who display early warning signs that they need help, receive compassionate effective support, it is less likely they will spiral downward. Furthermore, it would increase the chances for kindness, empathy, and respect for human life to cycle down throughout generations.

Currently in the United States, there are paralyzing political conflicts about guns. There is a large population that wants to exercise their right to arm themselves, and that is fine. I would guess the majority just want to protect their families. However, I believe organizations who advocate for weapons for self-defense should take action to police themselves, and provide ideas to prevent incidents because it is the disturbed people who use the weapons to take out precious innocent lives that sparks the outcry for gun control. In the wake of pain from unimaginable loss of innocent lives due to shootings, as a society, we need to collectively take steps to protect our children. Some of the people with the most protective instincts want to own guns to protect their families, and I am hoping they will use their protective instincts to protect all of our children.

I believe we can learn a lot from our children. I have learned so much from the children I have represented in the child welfare system. Children are so resilient, and can overcome so much pain if they have someone who genuinely cares about them and who believes in them. We need to listen to the voices of children because they have different perspectives and have wisdom to offer adults. In the United States, the CASA organization consists of court appointed special child advocates who volunteer to provide a voice for children in the child welfare system. If you live in the United States and would like to volunteer your time to provide a voice for an abused and neglected child in court, you may contact the CASA organization.

The child welfare system should be a solid quality safety net for abused and neglected children. For the child welfare system to help families maximize their potential, it is important that the safety and the best interests of the children guide recommendations and decisions. Politics, bureaucracy, corruption, and money should not guide. Professionals working in the child welfare system are working with lives in crisis, facing complex and difficult challenges, and to be effective, they must be empathetic with the families. The serious decisions will impact future generations. It is important for children to feel valued by our society as a whole.

Chapter 7

Exercises

1. **Blessings not burdens** – How can caretakers treat children as though they are blessings not burdens?

2. **Effect on children** – What do you believe are the likely short term and long term effects of children being treated as burdens?

3. **Self-discipline** – In what ways can you teach children the skills to have self-discipline, which minimizes the need to have authority provide the discipline?

4. **Making safe choices** – How can you teach children how to weigh the pros and cons to make safe choices in any situation they find themselves in?

5. **Special needs** – If a child has special needs, how would you obtain support for the child while building up the child's self-esteem so the child knows his or her worth? How would you ensure the child does not feel limited and defined by a label?

6. **Healthy relationships** – How do you teach children about the dynamics of a healthy relationship? In what ways could you teach children about the warning signs in determining unsafe people?

7. **Children in society** – Do you believe your country ensures children are a priority? If so, in what ways? If not, why? What changes would you like to see to help children maximize their potential?

NOTES

"My personal thoughts and feelings…"

NOTES

"My personal thoughts and feelings…"

"Love is the true essence of Life."

Chapter 8

Beyond Your Comfort Zone

How far have you traveled outside your comfort zone? Traveling outside our comfort zones may cause the people in our lives to pause and shake their heads; however, it is how we grow and truly live. Furthermore, it may prompt others to step out of their comfort zone and begin truly living the life they want. I have to admit, when it comes to leaving my comfort zone, I feel like I have traveled light years from it. (I am even shaking my head at this point.)

There is a difference between living to conform to the expectation of others, and allowing your life to blossom from the well of your soul. There are many people who allow fears to guide their lives. It is so easy for all of us to get caught up in the day-to-day tasks, and lose sight of the possibilities. When I say possibilities, it can be anything that is important to you. It may be being more vulnerable with a loved one. It may be coming out of hiding to face someone or something you have feared. It may be connecting to a person who meant a lot to you years ago, and you think of often, but make an excuse not to reconnect. It may be building up the nerve to talk to someone you feel connected to, but have not officially met. It could be following dreams that you pushed aside. It may be taking the trip you have wanted to take, but did not feel possible. Follow through with creating the invention you have put off completing. Change areas of employment. Climb the mountain you have always wanted to climb. It may be allowing yourself to follow your intuition. If you followed your heart and soul today, what is the worst that could happen? It is impossible to go through a door if it is not open. Someone may not open the door for you, so to make the impossible possible consider overcoming your fear by opening the door for yourself today.

Every person has his or her own comfort zone while discussing topics. It is important to remember that everyone comes from his or her own background, traditions, and experiences that may contribute to their own perceptions and beliefs. Some people do not question how they are taught while they are growing up; in comparison, there are some people who question everything they are told. When people have strong beliefs that they hold dear to them, they may feel it is a betrayal to ask questions, or to open their minds enough to consider beliefs that are to the contrary. If people feel emotionally safe to discuss topics openly through mutual respect, more ideas and beliefs may be exchanged with ease, and without pressure to conform either way. It is through the differing opinions, and discussing topics beyond our comfort zones, that growth and progress are allowed. Would we be so bold to make decisions today for people fifty years from now? I believe the answer would be no for most people, because the facts, circumstances, and events in life change on an ongoing basis, and people will need to weigh the facts while considering pros and cons based on the world events at that time. There are areas of our society where we are still relying on people who have passed away many years ago, and we still live according to their beliefs today, which may be beneficial for us, or in some cases, may not be applicable considering current events. Some do not even dare to raise questions because that would be a betrayal to their traditions and belief systems. Asking questions and discussing topics does not mean our minds and hearts must change positions, in fact, it may be personal confirmation; however, if we blindly believe without thinking for ourselves, we may miss the opportunity to improve. The truth is strong enough to withstand any questions and the test of time.

Chapter 8

Exercises

1. **Barriers** – Make a list of the fears creating barriers in the way of you leaving your comfort zone. Write down ways you could get around the barriers.

2. **Comfort zone** – How would you describe your comfort zone? How would you like your comfort zone to be in the future?

3. **Dreams** – Let's say anything is possible. Write down how your life would look five years from now if your dreams come true. Detail what steps you could take right now to make your dreams come true.

4. **Difficult topics** – What are some of your beliefs that you hold so dear that you would be reluctant to hear opinions that would contradict your beliefs?

5. **Asleep or awake?** – What are some areas in society where we tend to blindly believe without questioning?

NOTES

"My personal thoughts and feelings…"

NOTES

"My personal thoughts and feelings…"

_____
_____
_____
_____
_____
_____
_____
_____
_____
_____
_____
_____
_____
_____
_____
_____
_____

...~*♡*~...

Chapter 9

Intuition – Gift from the Divine

Honestly, I have contemplated whether or not to change the title of this chapter. At times, for me, intuition has not felt like a gift, but a nightmare. The human side of me would disagree with this, but deep within my soul I know the truth is that intuition is a divine gift. I believe intuition is the compass of the soul. All of us have intuition that may be utilized. Following intuition may be difficult at times because intuition may be guiding us in a direction that flows against the grain of society. Therefore, it complicates navigating life when the structure of the world we live in has difficulty receiving information that is not from a tangible source. I have been a skeptic throughout my life. I now find myself at a crossroads. Do I follow my heart and intuition, which upsets and hurts people I love for a period of time? Do I pretend that my intuition does not exist, and go through the motions? I know myself well enough that I cannot be fake. I have told my daughters to question everything they hear, and decide for themselves. Even though it forces my loved ones and I, outside of our comfort zones and down a rocky path, I am choosing to follow my heart and intuition because actions speak louder than words, and I feel it will be best for everyone in the future. The more we learn, the more we evolve as human beings. I believe in the people in my life, and I hope they will someday understand why I choose not to conform this time. We are all human, and if we ignore our intuition, heart, and feelings, then we lose ourselves.

How many people throughout history have been institutionalized or treated as if insane because they were sensitive to energies beyond what can be seen by the human eye? How many children have been institutionalized throughout history because society did not know how to handle them, and deemed them a risk? I do not know about you, but I have no idea what "normal" is, and I do not want to. I am going to share some of my intuitive experiences with you. I was going to use labels to describe different senses and experiences; however, I choose not to. I do not want to label because I do not want to narrow perceptions to understand the experiences. You may have explanations. It is in the exchange of different views that we achieve the greatest outcomes. I welcome you to place any labels you wish if it gives you more comfort; such as labels under the categories of metaphysical, scientific, or mental health.

It is by leaving our comfort zones that we discover the depth of us. I still wonder: are we born with a certain amount of intuition? Are intuitive experiences limited because we conform to the environment we live in? Is intuition heightened when people have to be more aware because they are living or working in unsafe conditions? What I will do is share experiences with you, and then you can decide for yourself because I am still in the learning process.

I still do not understand fully how intuition works, and I can assure you that I do not have all of the answers.

There are some people that will relate to the experiences. However, I want to acknowledge that for some of you, just like it was with me over the years, the experiences will challenge your comfort zone. It may be that you will feel the need to close down instead of being open, and that is fine. You need to decide what resonates with you, and I am in no way trying to impose my beliefs on anyone. I am merely sharing what I have experienced from my heart to yours.

Intuitive experiences occur on a regular basis; therefore, I cannot detail them all but I can provide examples of different types:

The first time I recall wondering how I knew something without having a basis is when I was approximately six years old. Actually, I may have been younger. I was in the backyard, and I heard some movement at the bottom of a metal tube. I looked in the tube, but everything was dark. Even though I could not see, I felt within that whatever was alive in the tube needed help and was not dangerous. I reached into the tube; meanwhile, my older brother yelled for me to stop because he was trying to protect me from what he thought might be a snake or other small animal. I remember when I heard him telling me to take my hand out, I had a strong feeling that I was supposed to help, and that there was no reason to fear. I continued to reach in and pulled out a little bird. I remember wondering, how did I know what was in the tube would not harm me? I did not have the words or the ability to comprehend what happened then.

Today, I believe it is likely I connected to the energy of the bird. However, I may be wrong.

I sometimes feel the energy of a person when I come in contact with him or her. I sometimes know things about them without having a basis. The following are a few examples:

I was working at my desk in California, many years ago, and a co-worker approached me from behind. Without turning around, I remember knowing who was approaching, and being overcome with a feeling of cancer. Since that feeling made me uncomfortable, and it startled me, I did not know what to do, so I just asked him if he had a physical recently, and encouraged him to do so. He was retiring and I assumed he would have wanted to enjoy his time with his family. Sadly, the cancer was too advanced, and he did not get to enjoy his retirement years as he wanted because the cancer took his life. For some reason, I seem to be more sensitive to cancer energy more than other diseases. It may be that working at the nursing home, as a teenager, fine-tuned my sensitivity in that area. I remember with some patients feeling that they had cancer, and with a few residents, the room smelled of an unpleasant odor, similar to burnt coffee, in the final stages.

I have also felt the spirit or energies of people who have passed away before. I remember one time, while living in California, I went to an event at a manager's home for employees in our office. I arrived and sat down to eat when I felt the spirit of a close friend pass by as if to say goodbye. I was stunned because this friend was sick in the hospital, but no one notified me that she had passed away. I calmly turned to a co-worker and apologized, indicating I had to leave because a dear friend passed away. While thoughts were running through my mind, I drove home. She had passed away around the time I felt her spirit, which the noted time of her passing was 6:00 pm, on July 23, 1987.

The first premonition I remember is when I was approximately eight or nine years old. I was sitting at the dining room table having dinner with aunts and uncles who were in town to visit. All of a sudden, I felt that the next time I would be sitting at the dining room table with my aunts and uncles would be because they are in town for my mother's funeral. I remember overwhelming sadness came over me. I excused myself and went to the bathroom and just cried thinking to myself, "This is silly, why can't I stop crying over something that hasn't happened?" Over eleven years later, the next time I was sitting in the same location, with my aunts and uncles, was the night before my mother's funeral. How is it possible that time and space can be linked so many years apart, or having a premonition for so many years into the future? Years ago, I had a premonition that someone dear to me would be married to a specific man she did not know at the time, and then she married him over twenty years later.

I have had premonitions over the years of people passing away. The following are a couple of examples:

In regard to my sister, while writing an email to a friend, I had the feeling my sister would be passing away, but there was nothing I could do about it. I felt it was too late. I did not tell my sister because I could not feel where, when, or how. I felt it was not meant for me to say anything because it would affect the quality of the remainder of her life. She passed away from a brain aneurysm. During the evening, after her passing, while we were talking to the donor coordinator, and the coordinator was describing how many people her donations will help, I heard my sister's voice clearly say, "How cool." Then later that evening, while walking past my nephew in the waiting room, and seeing him crying, I heard her voice again indicating that he should not cry because she is here and good. What really touched me the most is the feeling I had when I felt her presence, which was stronger than the words. Her spirit felt finally free, happy, and light.

I had a premonition, years ago, about a friend's youngest son passing away. Sadly, I did not know when, where, or how, I just had the feeling it would be soon. She called me and did not say a word. I am sure she was too upset to speak. I just stated "not", and then I stated her son's name, and she whispered, "Yes, he is gone." I immediately started to drive to her home so she would not be alone, and on the way I had a vision of him, and he had a message for his mother. I did not tell her that day. I waited because I knew she would not be ready to receive in the midst of her unspeakable grief. She went to his memorial out of the State, and I flew out to accompany her on the road trip back home so she did not have to drive alone during such a difficult time. On the road trip, I let her know about the premonition, and apologized that I did not have sufficient information so that she could warn her son. She surprised me, and told me that she had a premonition of him passing as well; however, she did not have enough information to warn him either.

She stated it had been haunting her up until his passing. I let her know her son's message and she understood the message even though I did not, at the time.

There have been circumstances when I felt intuitively that it was meant for me to try and help.

While attending college to obtain my Bachelor's degree, during a class, I had this feeling that one of the women in the classroom was feeling suicidal. She sat across the room, and I had never met her. I had a quick vision of her contemplating taking her life. I felt it was meant for me to reach out to her. After class, on the way out to the car, I had no idea what I was going to say, but I still approached her. The words just came out of me, "I know what you want to do. Please do not do it." She stopped and looked into my eyes, and she started crying. She asked me how I knew. I told her of the vision and the feeling I had. She indicated that her father recently passed away, and she had been close to him. She explained the night before she was thinking of suicide. I asked her if she would please accompany me inside to speak with the professor to see if she could help her. We walked inside and she did meet with the professor, and I left.

During my morning prayers, I was praying for a friend and her family, and I had a vision of her adult daughter with a little red haired boy. I really did not know her, except for meeting her once, and so I was surprised by the vision. I felt heaviness in my chest, and a desperate feeling that she and her husband are not meant to stop trying to have children. I called my friend and told her about this vision. She indicated that her daughter and son-in-law have been in too much pain because they had tried to have a baby for so many years, and so they decided to stop trying. She indicated that she was worried that telling her daughter about the vision may add to her pain. I told her that I have to call her because I know it is meant for her to get the message. I did speak with her. I sensed that her father, who had passed, may have been the source of my feeling. It is interesting that I felt heaviness in my chest while having the vision, and her father passed away from emphysema. Today, she has two beautiful boys, one is biological and the other adopted.

There have been times the facts appear contrary to my premonition.

The wedding and reception were set for an attorney in our office; however, I had a feeling she was meant to marry another specific man. The wedding was canceled for a different reason, but she did marry the man in the premonition. The same attorney in our law firm indicated to me that she just had an ultra sound and the doctor stated that she is having a boy. I responded, "No, I feel you are having a girl." She has a darling daughter.

There is a golden heart worth fighting for.

I have felt, for over four years, that a man, who I know, with a kind precious heart, is dying. He is a part of my heart and soul. I have never felt the depth of pain from anyone more than I have felt from him. I had a dream one night that he was sitting in his car on a country road, next to an emergency phone, feeling overwhelming despair. I felt he would need an organ transplant so I have tried to reach out in every way I could think of, so that he would ask me to donate. I even thought if I was completely vulnerable, and acted like a fool, maybe he would not be embarrassed to come to me. Since I do not know how energy works, I even put uplifting notes on the emergency phone on the country road in case my dream came true. Yes, I know it sounds crazy, but I am more concerned about his life than what people think of me.

To this day, he claims that he is in good health, his family is doing well, and does not need any help. When I met him, I felt the genuine kindness in the core of his heart and soul, and he is one of a kind. I have felt more sadness over the past four years, feeling like I am dying inside along with him, watching people walk by him and not seeing his pain. I believe he does not feel worthy to receive, which, if so, is tragic. Anyone who truly cares about him and loves him would want him to live. I know without a doubt it is meant for his light to shine in this world. I pray every day he will open his heart, and receive. Part of the reason I am writing this book is so that maybe he will realize his worth and live. I hope I am wrong, and that he is healthy and well. Again, his precious life is much more important than people thinking I am insane.

A sense of knowing when there is no basis of fact.

Sometimes when I have contact with people there is information that I know about them when there is no rational basis for the information. It happens on too many occasions to detail; however, there are a couple of occasions that particularly come to mind. The first time I met my spouse, in high school, I knew he was special, and I felt like I was meeting a part of my heart and soul. Even though we both moved away and did not have contact for years, I woke up one morning and knew that his mother had passed away, and he was having a difficult time grieving. In another special case, the first time I met a wonderful woman who has been a friend and, at times, a colleague, I knew instantly she was from a town I grew up in. I also knew she had been married twice, and I felt like I had known her for years. I had never met her prior to that first meeting.

While living in California, I received a phone call from a friend and colleague. I was still half asleep when I picked up the phone, and the radio was on. When I picked up the phone, I stated, "He didn't do it. It was the uncle." She was confused and just asked, "What?" Then, I apologized because I was half asleep and confused. Meanwhile, on the radio, they were reporting that a boy had killed his family. The uncle had claimed that his nephew had killed the family, and then he had to kill his nephew in self-defense. However, later within the next couple of weeks, I heard on the radio that the uncle is the one who had committed the homicides, and blamed his nephew.

Intuition as an investigative tool

I only base recommendations and decisions on credible evidence. While investigating, intuition can be a helpful tool if used responsibly because it is another sense. I am sure you have heard law enforcement or other professionals use the term gut feeling and that is what I am referring to when I am discussing using intuition as an investigative tool. The following are a couple of examples:

I have had feelings on occasions to conduct unannounced visits at times when I have felt kids are at risk, or when the parents are violating court orders. In addition, intuition is at times helpful in preventing kids from running, and locating runaways.

On one occasion, as an attorney for the best interests of abused and neglected children in the system, I pulled up to conduct a home visit, which was required to ensure the safety of the children. Prior looking up at the house while I was in my car, I had this overwhelming feeling of methamphetamines. I try to be very respectful of families when I am visiting because I understand that I am the one intruding in their home, and it is likely uncomfortable for them. I already decided that unless there was clear evidence I observed, I would ignore my feeling. Based on the smell of methamphetamines and other evidence, I called a caseworker experienced with substances and asked if she would conduct a visit to obtain a second opinion as to the safety of the home. The caseworker found evidence of a methamphetamines lab, and it turned out they had been dealing for years out of the home. I would not have mentioned what I suspected unless the caseworker found the evidence of the lab.

While representing the best interests of the children in the welfare system, there were times that I had to push my intuition aside because of lack of evidence. It was extremely difficult to intuitively feel that a case would reopen because of neglect or abuse in the future, but I could not object to closing the case because the evidence was not sufficient, at the time, to keep the case open.

Intuitive connections

It is possible to feel when people you are connected to are going through a difficult time. For example, on a couple of occasions, I have canceled the appointments for the rest of the work day because I felt it was meant for me to return home. On both occasions, one of my daughters had been injured in an accident. Also, when one daughter went to Ghana to volunteer to help orphans, I could feel her energy stronger from there than when she was at home, for some reason, and when I felt she was sick, I contacted her. I have also often felt when loved ones I am connected to are ill or going through a difficult time.

Dreams

Have you had intuitive dreams? I am not an expert in dream interpretation. However, there have been times that I have had realistic dreams that turned out to be true. The following are a couple of examples:

I had a reoccurring dream of a young child in a hospital room calling out for help for approximately two months. I received a case with a young child already in the hospital. I went to meet the child, and the child was the child calling out for help from my dream.

As I indicated in the introduction, I dreamed about a young girl who had been abducted, and the details were startling and seemed real. Despite my skepticism, I decided that morning to call into work and stay home for a few hours to search for the girl online. I decided at that moment no matter what the cost, including losing my job, if I confirmed the girl was actually missing, I would call in the details to the authorities. I could not find her in the news as missing, and I was relieved. I thought it was just a dream, and I threw the paper away. I was too busy in my life with my family and work to spend time dwelling on dreams. However, approximately one week later, on the National news, I saw a picture of the girl that had been abducted. I was saddened to realize she had been abused that entire time. My mind started racing. If I had only embraced my intuition years ago I may have been more advanced, and had been able to obtain details from the dream to help find the girl sooner.

Meditation and Prayers

I have heard people refer to praying as speaking to God or the divine, and meditation as receiving. I guess then when I connect to the divine; I am both sending and receiving. I envision the people I am praying for, and ask that any negative and/or ailments are removed from them, and envision that they are filled with love, light, and healing energy. I also pray that love and light surrounds and fills the world, after praying for specific people or groups. There are times when I feel if a person is having a difficult time, or if a person is feeling happy. I have also, at times, seen gray being cleared from people and, in rare instances, have seen a red spot in the vision, which I believe may reflect an ailment. It actually makes sense that connecting soul to soul; energy to energy, that information is shared.

Community Tragedies

I have often wondered why I have not had premonitions for natural disasters. I must not be in tune with natural disasters, or maybe I have not recognized the warning signs within myself prior to a natural disaster. There have been two occasions that I felt literally ill, and felt that a tragedy was going to take place. On the days of the Oklahoma bombing and the Columbine school tragedy, I felt literally ill with the feeling of impending doom, and turned on the TV just waiting for there to be an announcement. However, sadly, I did not know where, when, or what, until the media notified the public.

Auras

I am not sure if what I have seen would be classified as auras. I do not see colors around people; however, there have been times that I have seen light around people, or a grayish color on and around some people, at different times, especially if they are having some health issues or a lot of toxicity in their lives.

Spirits and Angels

I have only seen a few spirits of people who have passed on. My first experience was when I was washing the dishes, over twenty years ago, and I felt a presence behind me; meanwhile, the dog started barking, and turned around, and I briefly saw the mist of a woman with red hair and a red sweater, pass by me and disappear. All I can tell you is that my mother-in-law had red hair when she was alive, I was in the home she built, and the dog barking was her favorite dog. I feel it was likely her spirit, but I cannot say for sure. On another occasion, I was sleeping in a hotel room, and awoke to see the figure of a little blonde girl in a white nightgown standing next to me by the bed. I automatically thought it was my youngest daughter so I asked her what she needed, and closed my eyes again. When I did not hear her response, I opened my eyes and no one was there. I went into the connected hotel room and all four of our daughters were sound asleep. I wondered, was it my sister who had passed appearing young, or did the spirit have a connection to the hotel room? I do not know the answer. There was a time I was putting a cart away in the parking lot at a grocery store, and I saw a white mist spinning in a circle, and I did feel my sister's presence in that moment.

While I was working as a teen at a nursing home, prior to one of the residents passing away from cancer, she asked me if I saw the little boy waving to her. Yet, at a later date, in the same room, days prior to the passing of another resident from cancer, she asked me who the little boy is on the tricycle. The first time, I thought maybe the little boy appeared to welcome her to the other side, but then, two residents saw a little boy within days prior to dates of their passing, many months apart, but in the same room. It may have been the little boy had a connection to the room; however, I do not know. Then another resident in a different room, looking in the direction of the corner of the room, stated that there are people eating dinner and they want her to join them. She asked me if I wanted to join them as well, but I declined. She passed away within a week of having that vision. I cannot give you an explanation for what the residents experienced, all I can do is share them with you.

I mentioned that I have seen light around some people at different times. There have been times that I did not just see the light around them, but at the same time felt a presence that was there to help them. I believe in angels. In addition, there have been special human beings in my life who I consider Earth angels to me. Based on what I sense intuitively, I believe there are divine angels or, at times, loved ones who have passed on that come and support us during difficult times in our lives. *Divine love is limitless and the source of miracles.*

Before and/or after life?

Years ago, I had wondered how I knew so much about a friend without having any basis for the information. I prayed one time before going to bed that I would be guided to the answers. I dreamed I was with shimmering light beings that were in the outline shape of the human body, but without detailed features. Communication was telepathic. I remember thinking everything made sense about past lives, and I was amazed how at ease I felt. I had decided to go down to Earth to help a friend through some difficult times, the same friend I prayed about before going to sleep, as well as going down to help some other people. When I looked down at the Earth, there were lights. People who were emotionally connected had thriving bluish/silver threads between them, and the feeling I had was that the threads infused life. I woke up, and I have to tell you, I never felt that way before. It was so realistic, and I felt so awake. I do not know if it was a dream, or if that is how it will be after we transition to the other side. I can tell you that to me it feels like a memory, and not a dream. However, you need to believe what resonates with your soul. I wish I could give you all the gift of experiencing that dream for yourselves so that you could feel the loving calm that was apparent, and so that I could get your input so we could share thoughts about the experience.

Awakenings

I wish I was more comfortable with all of the above experiences I shared with you. I am in the process of learning and becoming more at ease. It should be an exciting exploration learning more from the vast world beyond what the human eyes can see. *The truth is that as complex human beings, with multisensory capabilities, we need to embrace our intuition in addition to logic, to be whole.*

Chapter 9

Exercises

1. **Intuition** – Have you had intuitive experiences? If so, recall some of the experiences. How did they impact you?

2. **Unexplained events** – Have you had any unexplained events in your life? If so, what were they? What are your thoughts about your experiences?

3. **Beyond this life** – Do you believe in before and/or afterlife? If so, what are your feelings?

4. **Faith** – Are you comfortable with believing in anything beyond what your eyes can see?

5. **Awakenings** – What are some awakenings you have had in your life? Would you like to become more awake? If so, in what ways?

6. **Incorporating intuition in your life** – How do you believe your intuition may help you in your future?

NOTES

"My personal thoughts and feelings…"

NOTES

"My personal thoughts and feelings…"

...~*♡*~...

Chapter 10

Compass of the Soul

"Intuition is the compass of the soul." To listen to intuition, we have to be open to our inner voice. Some people call it our conscience, following the spirit, or divine whispers. Do you feel you have followed your intuition in life?

To listen to your intuition, it is necessary to learn to distinguish if the source is from the ego or intuition. Have you ever felt an inner feeling to go in a certain direction, but you pushed the feeling aside and you're sorry you did not listen? It may be that you have this reoccurring feeling that you need to do something and you have no idea why, but the feeling will not go away, no matter how much you ignore it. I have found that important intuitive messages or guidance will not disappear until I have followed them, or it is too late. I have found if I do not listen to the soft nudges of divine whispers because they do not make sense to me; the nudges become firm shoves, and if I still do not listen then I get an unpleasant startling wake-up call while wishing I would have listened in the beginning. You can tell intuitive guidance because your intuition is the divine compass of your soul, and will only guide you to bring out the best within you, and to help, not harm others. *Intuition will guide you from a source of divine love.* However, it is still not easy to follow, because it may go against the grain of society, and maybe even against the beliefs of people you care about. In contrast, the ego often raises doubt about following your intuition while magnifying fears and anxiety.

Intuition is the gentle hand of divine love. I felt intuitively to write that intuition is the gentle hand of divine love. It is not a statement from me, but flowed through me. The statement holds greater wisdom than I possess. I have learned that the greatest wisdom comes when our souls are connected to the divine, and we allow information to flow through us without interference. It feels like I am merely a facilitator or a tool funneling information at times. It is possible I just had this experience for someone else who will read this book. When something resonates with our souls, it is confirmation within of what we already know to be true.

Our souls are drawn to certain people, places, or things for a reason. I feel in my heart and soul that I was drawn to becoming an attorney because there were people I was meant to connect with and help. Sometimes, we may not understand why we are drawn, and it may take years for the reasons to reveal themselves. For example, it may be you have felt like it is meant for you to go to a location and you have no idea why, but the feeling continues to swell up in you. It may be there is a special soul you are meant to connect to who will change your life, or it may be for a completely different reason. You will never know until you follow your intuition.

Intuition can help in every aspect of your life. I do believe that it is important to question ourselves, and our thoughts, on a daily basis to make sure we are not interpreting something wrong. Despite taking precautions, all of us make mistakes, and we will be wrong and fail at times, which is a part of the human experience. I have told our daughters after some of their sport games: winning is easy to handle, it is the response to losing that reflects the strength of character within. We often learn more from our failures and difficulties in life. Some days, I feel like putting my hands up in the air and saying I have learned enough, which I know is not true, but I would like to learn more from pleasant experiences in the future.

At our law firm, we obviously do not hire people without reviewing resumes, written material, calling references, conducting criminal background checks, and conducting interviews. However, one morning, many years ago, I called the office and asked if there is someone that contacted the firm for employment because I felt there is a specific person who is meant to join the team. At first, the team member indicated that she did not know of anyone. Then I received a call back, and I received the information that there actually was a woman who called a couple of times in the past about a job. I asked for her name and number. I contacted her and, as soon as she started speaking, I felt she was the soul that was meant to join our team. She had the same feeling that she was meant to work with us, and she did not know why. It surprised us both when I hired her over the phone. She still works at the law firm today, and she has not only put her heart and soul into helping children and families, she is a dear friend as well. If I did not go against the grain of the policy and procedures I put in place that day, then there are many children and families that would not have benefited from her exceptional work, and I would not have the trustworthy friend I have today. Intuition does not always coincide with rational thought.

In the midst of many people, there is an abundance of input; there are many energies, thoughts and feelings that may be absorbed. When I feel there is a lot of toxicity, if I remember, I will pray and picture divine love and light filling and surrounding the people and environment. On a daily basis, I pray to be filled with divine love and light, and that I be used as a tool to help others. I also pray that I will be guided to the people I am supposed to help. If there is going to be a meeting with difficult people, with the awareness that I can be difficult as well, sometimes I will pray prior to attending that ego not guide but that the most optimum outcomes are achieved.

Connection between the soul and divine

Every person is unique and has the ability to choose his or her own way to connect with the divine. For some people, religion may feel like a conduit to the divine, and other people may feel that religion interferes with a direct connection to the divine. Of course, there are some that do not wish to connect to the divine at all, or they may not even believe in a force greater than themselves. Meditation and praying are a couple ways that help to connect to the divine. However, I feel that I have developed more of an ongoing relationship, and so the communication, both ways, is random as long as I am open and not shut down. I do not hear voices. The communication and divine whispers I receive is through a sense of knowing, and the communication from me is through thoughts.

Nature streamlines my soul connection with the divine. The strong beautiful divine force of nature clears away my mental chatter, and steadies my soul. Intuition may flow while writing, speaking, driving, enjoying nature, gardening, and other activities. I find listening to music that resonates with my heart raises my vibrations and feeds my soul. When I am near water, it seems my intuition is more in tune. Also, lighting candles provides a calming environment for me to focus. The key is to find what resonates with you. Every person is unique and has the ability to find his or her own way to fine tune a personal intuitive flow.

Chapter 10

Exercises

1. **Intuition** – Have you followed your intuition in life? If so, in what ways? Have you pushed your intuition away? If so, in what ways?

2. **Fine tuning intuition** – When do you feel you are most in tune with your intuition? What helps you fine tune the connection between your soul and the divine?

3. **Divine whispers** – Is there a feeling in you that has been cycling for a period of time to guide you in a direction? If so, have you followed it? What was the outcome? If not, what barriers are in the way of you following the guidance? What steps could you take to follow your intuitive guidance?

4. **Divine flow of knowledge** – Have you felt messages flow through you while speaking, or writing, which reflect greater wisdom? If so, did you pass the messages on?

NOTES

"My personal thoughts and feelings…"

NOTES

"My personal thoughts and feelings…"

Chapter 11

Humanity

What would the world be like today if every single human being felt physically and emotionally safe to be his or her true self? Just think of the limitless possibilities if human beings cared more about lifting each other up instead of breaking each other down.

Human rights

I get extremely angry when I think about the human rights atrocities throughout the history of civilization. As individuals, a country, and a world family, we need to take responsibility and find ways to eliminate human rights violations. Every time there is an injustice to one of us it impacts all of us. We are failing worldwide to value all human life. We cheat ourselves, and deplete our level of character as a whole every time we minimize the value of another life due to any physical feature, race, gender, and/or relationship. I cannot comprehend why some people gain pleasure from hurting and pushing others down. *The character of society coincides with how we treat our most vulnerable people.* I must admit, I have had many moments, especially after watching the news, that I have become skeptical, and began losing hope for humanity until some kind person or kind act restores my faith in the human spirit. If we treat people like they are inferior, and like they are worth nothing, often they become hurt, angry, and may even reach out for ways to numb the pain, which has an impact on our society as a whole.

What does the soul of your political system resonate?

In my opinion, democracy is the optimum political structure, as it values the voices of the people. However, I believe corruption still exists in politics to the point many people become indifferent. Political conflict appears to hinder government leaders from making timely and effective decisions. Most people can learn about the different issues affecting a country; however, a genuine leader, even while in the midst of political turmoil, will have the courage to make decisions from a foundation of ethics, empathy, and genuine concern. Money has too much influence in politics and contributes to an imbalance in power. In my opinion, political leaders should work hard to ensure that people remain the priority above political tactics and conflict. The political environment today seems to be more focused on tearing down other political parties and leaders rather than coming together with mutual respect to serve humanity. Political leaders have the choice to conform to mediocrity, or go against the grain when necessary, to truly make a positive difference and become a part of the solution. Political leaders have the ability to make the choice to collaborate, to develop, and implement timely creative plans to move the country forward in a positive direction or remain stagnant.

Effective leadership

Leaders, in general, can choose to lead through fear and intimidation, or they can decide to lead through actions guided by empathy and character. If a person is in a position with the illusion of power over others, it is easier but inhumane to control by fear, and reflects weakness rather than strength in leadership. Furthermore, it creates an environment that does not allow people to maximize their strengths and their potential, which prevents all involved from thriving. In comparison, effective leadership will respect the individual strengths, and appreciate the importance of the unique contribution from every team member. Furthermore, an effective leader will not be threatened by new ideas but will welcome input. Regardless, if it is at school, work, or church every person can be a leader in his or her life by setting an example and by caring enough to attempt to achieve the optimum outcomes for all involved.

Soul of the workplace

Despite what jobs we hold, *caring* is essential for quality work in any area. Many people can feel if someone is genuine and truly cares. Whether it is a customer you are serving, or whether you are a politician serving constituents, the level of sincerity can often be felt. I believe every person should ask themselves if they are helping or harming in the position they hold. Every person is different, and it is a personal decision to care or not care, which is fine; however, a person who does not care would hopefully decide to work in an area that does not affect lives in a substantial manner.

For one example, it is essential that people working in the child welfare system sincerely care about the children to achieve optimum outcomes for the children and families. The safety of the children our firm represents in the child welfare system is our first priority, and we still receive calls from kids we represented years ago, which we enjoy. The children, who are old enough to understand, can feel if we are merely going through the motions because it is a job, or if we truly care about their wellbeing. Children can often feel if foster parents take them into the home for pay, compared to a heartfelt welcoming into their home. A child may feel if a caseworker or attorney is merely going through the motions. If abused and neglected children feel worthless and like a number within the system that is trying to protect them, then their self-esteem, level of confidence, and behaviors will likely coincide with how they are treated.

For another example, in our law firm, we also handle dissolution of marriage cases. Dissolving a marriage can be one of the most traumatic times in the lives of our clients. The clients make the final decisions; however, we encourage whenever possible to consider minimizing conflict, when appropriate, so that this traumatic time does not define his or her future. We are concerned about the present as well as the future for our clients and their children. In the midst of dissolving a marriage, it is so easy to allow their anger to guide in such a difficult time, and to want to hurt the other side to the point thought process becomes irrational. When the toxicity guides, then futures may be destroyed.

We encourage our clients to consider his or her best interests as well as the best interests of his or her children when weighing the pros and cons of their decisions. We also often encourage our clients to try to envision the difficult time as a door to redesigning their future instead of creating a foundation for years of conflict and emotional pain.

Acts of kindness

The far reaching ripple effect from an act of kindness can be immeasurable. When we come in contact with other precious lives, we do not know what trials they are going through and the challenges they face. It may be a person is suffering deep loss, or feeling hopeless. It may be something as simple as a kind word or a simple kind deed that may make a huge difference in the life of another person. In addition, he or she may be inspired to pass on the kindness to another person.

There are many people who feel completely alone, and feel invisible. We are all connected, and have the same desire to be treated with respect and compassion. Indifference and lack of concern for other human beings is contagious; empathy and kindness are contagious as well. *Every person has the choice to contribute to or drain from this world.*

Soul of our world

No one person can solve all of the problems in the world. It takes empathetic people with strong character from all around the world to find creative and compassionate solutions where they live, which contributes to the soul of our world.

Chapter 11

Exercises

1. **Human rights violations** – What are the human rights violations that concern you most at this time? What do you believe are some ways we could stop these human rights violations from occurring?

2. **Vulnerable populations** – What populations do you believe are the most vulnerable? Do you make a point to see people who are vulnerable or struggling? What can we do to help raise awareness and help?

3. **Acts of kindness** – What are some of the kind acts you have done for other people? Would you be willing to commit to yourself to at least one act of kindness a day or a week? If so, what can you do?

4. **Soul of our world** – How do you feel you may contribute to the soul of our world?

5. **Humanitarian leadership** – What can you do to reflect leadership by setting an example in your daily life to contribute to raising the level of humanity?

Humanity

...~*♡*~...

NOTES

"My personal thoughts and feelings…"

NOTES

"My personal thoughts and feelings…"

...~*♡*~...

Chapter 12

Soul Print

There are endearing people who come into our lives and leave a soul print. I feel people have their own unique soul signatures. Soul prints may even be made with a brief encounter, and then, there are some loved ones that leave prints over a lifetime. There are soul prints that are instant and deep, like first time I looked into the eyes of each one of my daughters. In my life, there have been people who have left soul prints with such depth that they will be a part of my heart and soul forever.

I believe soul messages are shared with each other as we are all connected, whether individually or collectively; such as messages that are emitted from organizations, churches and countries. What soul messages do we send? Our actions and intent guide whether those messages are sent from the best part of us, or our weaknesses. If messages are sent from our heart and souls, then it maximizes the opportunity for the best outcomes. If we send messages filtered through hate, anger, or fears, then we can expect the worst outcomes.

Nature I believe is one of the most precious living divine soul prints in this world. Furthermore, nature seems to have a special ability to leave an individual print within each one of us. One of my favorite words is beautiful. The word beautiful to me describes a sense and how I feel in the presence of greatness. For example, the beautiful feeling I have in the presence of the ocean. *Nature is a beautiful divine force of artistic expression infusing love into the soul.*

There are many artists that create from the well of their souls. Artwork may connect emotionally with people on a deep level. It feels like the soul signature of some artists, whether drawing, painting, songs, or other art forms, can travel through their work. It is a reminder to me that what we do matters. Our world is wealthier because of our differences and our unique contributions. The unique soul signatures of all human beings together make up the soul of our world.

To all of you who have never felt genuine love, may you find the love and light inside you, and may you have the courage to treat others with kindness and leave beautiful soul prints. Our real lasting legacies are the prints we leave in the hearts of others and on the soul of our world.

Chapter 12

Exercises

1. **Endearing people in your life** – List some of the people who have left soul prints in your life. In what ways have they left a print? Have you let the people, who have made a positive soul print in your life, know how much you care about them? If not, do you plan to let them know?

2. **Soul connections** – Have you ever felt a soul connection with another person? If so, who? How has it impacted your life? What soul message do you feel you give out to the world? What soul message do you think your country sends out to the world?

3. **Soul to soul connections** – Have there been any circumstances that you felt soul signatures or energy from another? If so, when and how? Have you ever felt that you and someone else communicate soul to soul? If so, who and describe some examples.

4. **Your soul prints** – List some ways you believe you have made soul prints in the lives of others. When you leave this world, what soul print on the world do you want to leave?

NOTES

"My personal thoughts and feelings…"

NOTES

"My personal thoughts and feelings…"

"The threads of logic, intuition, and humanity should be beautifully interwoven through the fabric of our world."

...~*♡*~...

Quotes
by Leta B.

"The character of society coincides with how we treat our most vulnerable members of society."

"There are endearing people who come into our lives and leave a soul print."

"Nature is a beautiful divine force of artistic expression infusing love into our souls."

"As we discover the vast possibilities beyond what our human eyes can see, we must be responsible and use our discoveries to bring out the best in our world or the discoveries are worthless."

"Love is the true essence of Life."

"The threads of logic, intuition, and humanity should be beautifully interwoven through the fabric of our world."

"Children are blessings not burdens in our families, our society, and in our world."

*"Education is a doorway for children
to maximize their potential."*

*"Nature streamlines the soul connection
with the divine."*

*"Souls are unique divine signatures of pure love
that existed before physical form, and will continue
to exist after our physical containers are shed."*

"Intuition is the gentle hand of divine love."

*"May you let the authentic colors of your heart illuminate
and may you feel the light within others."*

*"If a path in your life leaves you in a place where you feel
lost and alone, may you follow your heart and soul
until you feel at home."*

*"The simple truth is that every human being should be
born with basic human rights without suffering
from discrimination."*

*"If as a society we place more value on people
for their physical appearance; such as weight, skin, eye
color, and height, versus their heart and character,
then we are draining the wealth and heart
out of our society."*

"May you have the courage to choose love over hate."

*"Transform your anger into energy to effectuate
positive change."*

*"Until you align your mind with your soul,
you will continue to grieve for your highest self."*

*"As you step out of your comfort zone,
may life embrace you back."*

"Intuition is the compass of the soul."

"Prejudice is poison in the veins of the world."

"Divine love is limitless and the source of miracles."

*"Children will often rise or fall according
to the expectations of loved ones in their lives."*

*"Today, is the beginning of your future
so be as creative as your heart desires in designing
your life map."*

*"There is a vast existence beyond what our eyes can see,
and if we close our minds we limit our possibilities."*

*"If a rare golden heart is sacrificed in the process
of trying to research or help many,
then the world loses."*

*"The soul is steady just waiting to be fed
and to blossom."*

"Transform hurt and pain into peace and blessings."

*"No one has the ability to define who you are
unless you give permission."*

*"Every precious human being born should have
the right to live, love, and maximize his or her potential
without suffering from discrimination."*

*"It is a divine gift to find the light inside
in the midst of despair."*

*"Everyone leaves this Earth at some time,
and it is essential that we remind each other to cherish
and honor the lives of our loved ones rather than focusing
on the manner they left this world."*

*"Every person has the choice to contribute to or drain
from this world."*

*"To be whole, we need to embrace both
intuition and logic."*

*"Our real lasting legacies are the prints we leave
on the soul of the world."*

*"There is no better soil than real love for a heart
to blossom and truly live."* – Lisa Kimz

...~*♡*~...

Your Steady Soul

...~*♡*~...

Thank you all for sharing this journey with me, and may you be filled with peace, joy and blessings as you follow your own unique life map. May the love and the colorful light I am intending to send to you through this book reach your heart, and may you share love and light with others.

...~*♡*~...

...~*♡*~...

Helpful Information

If you would like additional information regarding fetal alcohol spectrum disorders, please contact the following National organization in the United States:

National Organization on Fetal Alcohol Syndrome ("NOFAS")
Office: (202) 785-4585 or (800) 66-NOFAS
Website: www.nofas.org

If you are currently living in a relationship involving domestic violence, the following is a number you may call for help:

The National Domestic Violence Hotline
Office: 1 (800) 799-SAFE(7233)
Website: www.thehotline.org

If you would like to be a volunteer child advocate in the United States for abused and neglected children in the child welfare system, please contact the following:

National CASA Association of Court Appointed Special Advocates ("CASA")
Office: 1 (800) 628-3233
Website: www.casaforchildren.org